The American Collection

VICTORIAN

165 New House Plans with Historic Elegance

Welcoming Porches, Fine Details, Comfortable Living Spaces

The American Collection
VICTORIAN

Published by Hanley Wood
One Thomas Circle, NW, Suite 600
Washington, DC 20005

Distribution Center
PBD
Hanley Wood Consumer Group
3280 Summit Ridge Parkway
Duluth, Georgia 30096

Vice President, Home Plans, Andrew Schultz
Associate Publisher, Editorial Development, Jennifer Pearce
Managing Editor, Hannah McCann
Editor, Simon Hyoun
Assistant Editor, Kimberly Johnson
Publications Manager, Brian Haefs
Production Manager, Melissa Curry
Director, Plans Marketing, Mark Wilkin
Senior Plan Merchandiser, Nicole Phipps
Plan Merchandiser, Hillary Huff
Graphic Artist, Joong Min
Plan Data Team Leader, Susan Jasmin
Marketing Director, Holly Miller
Marketing Manager, Brett Bryant

Most Hanley Wood titles are available at quantity discounts
with bulk purchases for educational, business, or sales
promotional use. For information, please contact Andrew Schultz
at aschultz@hanleywood.com.

BIG DESIGNS, INC.
President, Creative Director, Anthony D'Elia
Vice President, Business Manager, Megan D'Elia
Vice President, Design Director, Chris Bonavita
Editorial Director, John Roach
Assistant Editor, Carrie Atkinson
Senior Art Director, Stephen Reinfurt
Production Director, David Barbella
Production Manager, Rich Fuentes
Photo Editor, Christine DiVuolo
Graphic Designer, Frank Augugliaro
Graphic Designer, Billy Doremus

PHOTO CREDITS
Front Cover, Main: Design HPK2800100 on page 99.
Photo by Bob Greenspan.
Front Cover, Inset: Design HPK2800001 on page 6. Photo by Chris Little
Back Cover, Top: Design HPK2800002 on page 8.
Photo by Bob Greenspan.

10 9 8 7 6 5 4 3 2 1

Printed in the United States of America

Library of Congress Control Number: 2006925826
ISBN-13: 978-1-931131-67-4
ISBN-10: 1-931131-67-8

Contents

6 History Preserved
A dynamic exterior touched with period trimmings

8 Revival Study
Romanesque features with a strong, stone finish

11 Homes Under 1,800 Sq. Ft.
Victorian essentials for the small family

43 Homes From 1,800-2,499 Sq. Ft.
The distinctive look in traditional sizes

97 Homes More Than 2,500 Sq. Ft.
The Victorian home, at large

184 How To Order Blueprints

ONLINE EXTRA!

Hanley Wood Passageway

The Hanley Wood Passageway is an online search tool for your home plan needs! Discover even more useful information about building your new home, search additional new home plans, access online ordering, and more at www.hanleywoodbooks.com/acvictorian

THE ROYAL HOUSE

A brief history of the Victorian home

A traditional, two-story turret with detailed carvings and designs help make this home distinctly Victorian.

Named for Queen Victoria, during whose reign the style reached the peak of its popularity, Victorian architecture comprises a number of substyles, including Gothic Revival, Queen Anne, Second Empire, Richardsonian Romanesque, Shingle, Stick, and Folk. All these seemingly disparate styles embraced the 19th-Century Romantic ideal of a "natural" environment for domestic life: homes with graceful, expressive detailing that complemented the forms of nature and rejected strict geometry and Classical structure. Still, later variations of the Victorian style more freely borrowed from Medieval and Classical precedents.

From the outside, this family home's Victorian influence is apparent. Turn to page 117 to see what's inside.

Home as Progress

As with other architectural movements, it was technical innovation that enabled creative vision to become reality. New industrial methods allowed lumber to be milled more quickly and cheaply, and to be transferred all over the country via a modern railway network. Other steam-powered machines, such as scroll saws and shapers, enabled the mass production of the now-familiar Victorian features: exuberant flourishes, multitextured walls, complex roof shapes, turrets and bays, and elaborate window surrounds. Finally, the efficiently produced Victorian home could be affordably larger than earlier designs framed in heavy timber, bringing to the middle class a level of luxury previously enjoyed only by the wealthy.

The same expansion of industry that enabled Victorian architecture had a dramatic effect on the life of the Victorian family. As factory jobs, railroads, and other sources of employment required working family members to spend most of the day away from the home, the home itself evolved to accommodate those that stayed behind. Where earlier architectural styles may have been committed to abstract principals of a guiding aesthetic, the Victorian home placed more emphasis on the practical demands of domestic life, becoming a true work-at-home home.

The Victorian, Today

The plans collected in this book represent the culmination of that desire for a functional and beautiful home. Behind their delicately crafted exteriors, these homes feature open layouts that respond to casual family gatherings as well as serve hosted affairs. Formal and shared spaces cluster together while private rooms find comfortable distance away from one another. The multi-car garage has been designed to fit the rest of the home, providing a modern convenience without compromising the historically informed facade. Lastly, all plans allow for the most up-to-date home automation systems.

How to Use This Book

Following this introduction, our featured homes section will take you on a tour of two designs that exemplify the Victorian home. Take time to visualize the flow of interior spaces and imagine how these homes—and others like them—would feel to you. The rest of the book is divided into three sections and ordered by square footage.

Every plan discussed in this book is available to own. Turn to page 184 to learn how to order a plan and what you will receive with your purchase. Materials lists, customization, home automation, and other options are also explained in this part of the book, followed by the list of prices on page 190.

HISTORY PRESERVED

A dynamic exterior touched with period trimmings

The windowed turret and roof cresting are prominent Victorian features.

A circular front room with a wraparound porch, a conical tower, and gingerbread trim all add to the overall attraction of this Victorian home. The porch ends at a broad covered entrance. The dramatic, spacious great room features a vaulted ceiling, semicircular roof monitor, and diagonally placed corner fireplace. The extraordinary kitchen includes angled counters, a corner sink, center island with space for informal dining, and an airy breakfast nook with French doors to the patio. Entrance to the wonderful first-floor master suite is through angled double doors. A high tray ceiling, large walk-in closet, and dressing alcove are featured. A gorgeous compartmented bath is bathed in sunlight from two glass-block walls, and includes a whirlpool tub and double vanity.

plan# HPK2800001

First Floor: 1,960 sq. ft.
Second Floor: 736 sq. ft.
Total: 2,696 sq. ft.
Bedrooms: 4
Bathrooms: 3
Width: 69' - 2"
Depth: 50' - 2"
Foundation: Crawlspace, Slab,
Unfinished Basement

ORDER ONLINE @ EPLANS.COM

Bottom Right: A tile fireplace slip and iron accessories are in tune with the home's Victorian design. **Above:** An encompassing bay of windows keeps the dining room bright while delicate lace curtains keep it elegant. **Top Right:** Fine period details surround the front porch and entryway.

FIRST FLOOR

MSTR BATH
WICL
STOR
UTIL
CL
AUN RM
BATH
CL
T.V./GUEST RM
13'-4" x 11'-8"
TWO CAR GARAGE
20'-0" x 20'-6"
TRAY CEIL
MSTR BEDRM
17'-4" x 15'-0"
KITCHEN
ISLAND
19'-2" x 15'-4"
BKFST RM
PANT
OV REF
DN TO OPT BSMT
UP
2 STORY CEIL
FOYER
COV PORCH
RAIL
VAULTED
GREAT RM
15'-0" x 26'-0"
VAULTED
DINING RM
15'-8" x 12'-2"

SECOND FLOOR

UPPER MSTR BEDRM
WICL
BATH
BEDRM #3
13'-8" x 13'-6"
BALC
DN
RAIL
WICL
BEDRM #2
13'-6" x 10'-2"
REC RM
10'-4" x 18'-0"
DOME CEIL
UPPER FOYER

REVIVAL STUDY
Romanesque features with a strong, stone finish

Colorful gingerbread details, fish-scale roofing, and turned-wood spindles make this exterior undeniably Victorian.

Queen Anne houses, with their projecting bays, towers, and wraparound porches, are the apex of the Victorian era. This up-to-date rendition of the beloved style captures a floor plan that is as dramatic on the inside as it is on the outside. The front-facing pediment ornamented with typical gable detailing highlights the front doorway and provides additional welcome to this enchanted abode. The angles and bays that occur in every first-floor room add visual excitement to formal and informal living and dining areas. A well-lit breakfast bay with its soaring ceiling is a spectacular addition to this classic plan. The first-floor master suite features two walk-in closets. Three upstairs bedrooms also have spacious walk-in closets.

Above: This interior decor is as authentic to the time as the front facade, with stained-glass window accents, lace curtains, and tile flooring. Right: A wooden screen in the pass-through to the living room is a typical ornament of Victorian style.

plan # HPK2800002

First Floor: 1,600 sq. ft.
Second Floor: 790 sq. ft.
Total: 2,390 sq. ft.
Bedrooms: 4
Bathrooms: 3½
Width: 45' - 0"
Depth: 54' - 0"
Foundation: Crawlspace

ORDER ONLINE @ EPLANS.COM

While the design may be turn-of-the-century, the conveniences are all modern in the master bath.

FIRST FLOOR

SECOND FLOOR

HOMES UNDER 1,800 SQUARE FEET

For new families and couples just starting out, there are few better homes than Victorian homes. Designed to be economical and attractive, early Victorians brought ornate detailing and high style to the average American homeowner. The result was a home that provided formal entertaining spaces in even small homes, while preserving comfortable private quarters for the family.

Because of the designs' modest square footage, these homes include inventive spacing and storage solutions perfect for small families. A partition between the living and dining rooms is the perfect spot for built-in shelves and cabinets. Use under-stair storage in lieu of basements and attics. Make the best use of seasonal spaces, such as covered porches and bayed areas. In smaller homes, homeowners should have no trouble getting natural light to reach all parts of the home.

You'll be surprised at how much can fit into a plan less than 1,800 square feet. Plan versatility allows bedrooms to become home offices; the dining room can double as breakfast space; you can use bonus rooms for media rooms, game rooms, or an extra bedroom; and don't forget about all of the alfresco dining possibilities on decks and patios. Building a smaller home doesn't necessarily mean settling for less. It just means creatively using space to give yourself more: The Victorian homes in this section can do just that.

An elevated breakfast room, with 16-foot ceilings, brightens the heart of this small-family design. **See more of HPK2800036 on page 42.**

This romantic cottage design is ideal for any countryside setting. Lively Victorian details enhance the exterior. A wrapping porch with a gazebo-style sitting area encourages refreshing outdoor relaxation; interior spaces are open to each other. The kitchen with a snack bar is open to both the dining area and the living room. A powder bath with laundry facilities completes the first floor. The second floor offers space for three family bedrooms with walk-in closets and a pampering whirlpool bath.

plan # HPK2800003

First Floor: 960 sq. ft.
Second Floor: 838 sq. ft.
Total: 1,798 sq. ft.
Bedrooms: 3
Bathrooms: 1½
Width: 36' - 0"
Depth: 30' - 0"
Foundation: Unfinished Basement

ORDER ONLINE @ EPLANS.COM

14'-4" X 14'-0"
4,30 X 4,20

20'-4" X 13'-8"
6,10 X 4,10

12'-10" X 15'-0"
3,85 X 4,50

FIRST FLOOR

11'-8" X 11'-8"
3,50 X 3,50

10'-0" X 13'-0"
3,00 X 3,90

12'-6" X 15'-4"
3,75 X 4,60

SECOND FLOOR

HELPFUL HINT! | Modify your plan with our easy-to-use customization service.

plan# HPK2800004

First Floor: 840 sq. ft.
Second Floor: 757 sq. ft.
Total: 1,597 sq. ft.
Bedrooms: 3
Bathrooms: 3
Width: 26' - 0"
Depth: 32' - 0"
Foundation: Unfinished Basement

ORDER ONLINE @ EPLANS.COM

The amazing turret/gazebo porch on this classy home has an authentic Victorian flavor. Exceptional details accent this classic view. The bedroom on the first level offers a protruding balcony, which adds appeal both inside and outside. The entrance leads to the living room, located just left of the dining area and L-shaped kitchen. The master suite features a walk-in closet and a private bath with dual sinks. Two more family bedrooms are located on the second level.

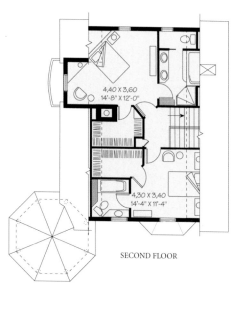

SECOND FLOOR

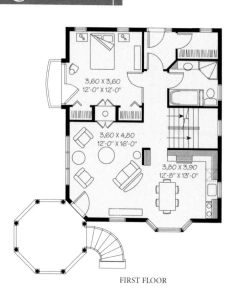

FIRST FLOOR

The charming front porch and the two-story turret welcome guests to this lovely home. The turret houses the living room on the first floor and the master suite on the second floor. The dining room is open to the living room and provides a box-bay window. The L-shaped kitchen features a breakfast room accessible to the backyard. A curved staircase next to the powder room leads upstairs to three bedrooms and a bath. Each family bedroom contains a walk-in closet.

plan# HPK2800005

First Floor: 805 sq. ft.
Second Floor: 779 sq. ft.
Total: 1,584 sq. ft.
Bedrooms: 3
Bathrooms: 1½
Width: 25' - 0"
Depth: 36' - 0"
Foundation: Unfinished Basement

ORDER ONLINE @ EPLANS.COM

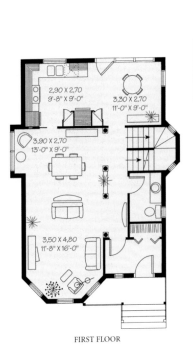

FIRST FLOOR

SECOND FLOOR

plan# HPK2800006

First Floor: 754 sq. ft.
Second Floor: 754 sq. ft.
Total: 1,508 sq. ft.
Bonus Space: 275 sq. ft.
Bedrooms: 3
Bathrooms: 1½
Width: 36' - 0"
Depth: 35' - 6"
Foundation: Unfinished Basement

ORDER ONLINE @ EPLANS.COM

Making a grand entrance through this sophisticated entry is a treat. Windows wrap around the outside of the turret. A closet greets guests and homeowners inside the entry. The living room is well lit and opens to the dining room. A conveniently placed bathroom resides to the left of the dining room. Rear-porch access is off the breakfast nook where windows allow light to flood both the kitchen and nook. Another window over the kitchen sink brightens the chef's work area even more. Two family bedrooms and one master bedroom are located on the second floor for sleeping comfort.

SECOND FLOOR

FIRST FLOOR

This country Victorian design comes loaded with charm and amenities. The entry leads to open living space, defined by a two-sided fireplace and a large bay window. An island counter with a snack bar highlights the L-shaped kitchen. A quiet sitting area opens to the outdoors. Upstairs, the master suite allows plenty of sunlight from the turret's bay window and boasts a step-up tub, dual-sink vanity, and separate shower. Bonus space above the garage offers room for future expansion.

plan# HPK2800007

First Floor: 880 sq. ft.
Second Floor: 880 sq. ft.
Total: 1,760 sq. ft.
Bonus Space: 256 sq. ft.
Bedrooms: 3
Bathrooms: 2½
Width: 42' - 0"
Depth: 40' - 0"
Foundation: Unfinished Basement

ORDER ONLINE @ EPLANS.COM

FIRST FLOOR

SECOND FLOOR

plan # HPK2800008

First Floor: 778 sq. ft.
Second Floor: 810 sq. ft.
Total: 1,588 sq. ft.
Bedrooms: 3
Bathrooms: 1½
Width: 38' - 0"
Depth: 35' - 0"
Foundation: Unfinished Basement

ORDER ONLINE @ EPLANS.COM

This lovely two-story home draws heavily on the Queen Anne period with the covered porch that encompasses the lower half of the nested tower. Flanking the foyer on the right is the entertaining family room—great for gatherings. The gourmet kitchen enjoys plenty of counter space and is open to the breakfast area which accesses the rear porch. Completing this floor is a powder room with a utility room nearby. The second floor holds two family bedrooms and a luxurious master suite, all sharing a full bath that includes an oversized pampering tub—note the master bedroom accesses the bath through its own private pocket door.

FIRST FLOOR

3,60 X 6,80
12'-0" X 22'-8"

3,00 X 3,60
10'-0" X 12'-0"

3,00 X 4,00
10'-0" X 13'-4"

3,90 X 4,50
13'-0" X 15'-0"

SECOND FLOOR

3,40 X 3,00
11'-4" X 10'-0"

3,00 X 3,80
10'-0" X 12'-8"

3,60 X 4,50
12'-0" X 15'-0"

3,90 X 4,50
13'-0" X 15'-0"

HELPFUL HINT! Reproducible plans are your best value. You can make as many as you need.

©The Sater Design Collection, Inc.

This intriguing home is full of elegant Victorian detail and many amenities. Beyond the grand staircase and central foyer are the living areas; on the left is the dining room and on the right is the kitchen, which provides plenty of counter space and a pantry. The great room includes a fireplace and built-in cabinets. Toward the front of the first floor is a family bedroom with a private bath, a utility room, and a powder room. The master suite (with a master bath) and a loft open to the great room below and dominate the second floor.

plan# HPK2800009

First Floor: 1,143 sq. ft.
Second Floor: 651 sq. ft.
Total: 1,794 sq. ft.
Bedrooms: 2
Bathrooms: 2½
Width: 32' - 0"
Depth: 57' - 0"
Foundation: Island Basement

ORDER ONLINE @ EPLANS.COM

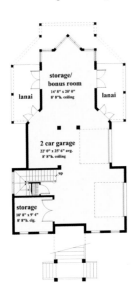

FIRST FLOOR

SECOND FLOOR

plan# HPK2800010

First Floor: 805 sq. ft.
Second Floor: 758 sq. ft.
Total: 1,563 sq. ft.
Bedrooms: 3
Bathrooms: 2½
Width: 49' - 0"
Depth: 37' - 8"
Foundation: Crawlspace

ORDER ONLINE @ EPLANS.COM

Perfect for narrow lots, this practical, smaller home is a builder's dream. Ideal for a first home, it offers an open layout that adds a feeling of spaciousness. A fireplace on the first floor warms the family room, breakfast area, and kitchen. Upstairs houses the master suite, two family bedrooms, and a full bath. The laundry room is conveniently located on the second floor with the bedrooms.

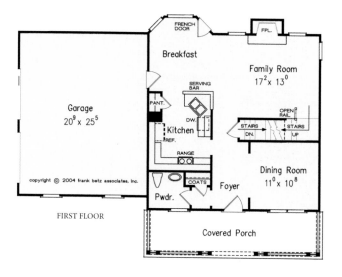

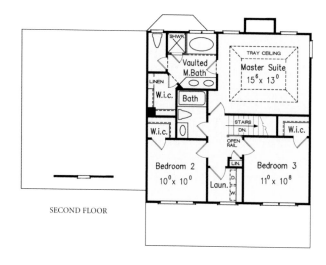

THIS HOME, AS SHOWN IN THE PHOTOGRAPH, MAY DIFFER FROM THE ACTUAL BLUEPRINTS. FOR MORE DETAILED INFORMATION, PLEASE CHECK THE FLOOR PLANS CAREFULLY.

PHOTOGRAPHY COURTESY OF MCGUIRE GROUP ARCHITECTS

A wraparound porch introduces this practical design that's full of amenities. Windows open up the living room on three sides to let in natural light and let you keep an eye on kids playing on the porch. The U-shaped kitchen opens to the bright breakfast room. A spacious dining room and a powder room complete the first floor. The second floor offers the master suite—with a walk-in closet and private bath—and two family bedrooms that share a hall bath.

plan# HPK2800011

First Floor: 832 sq. ft.
Second Floor: 789 sq. ft.
Total: 1,621 sq. ft.
Bedrooms: 3
Bathrooms: 2½
Width: 44' - 0"
Depth: 32' - 0"
Foundation: Crawlspace, Unfinished Basement

ORDER ONLINE @ EPLANS.COM

Breakfast
9'-4" x 8'-0"

Utility

Kitchen
9'-4" x 10'-8"

Living Rm.
12'-2" x 15'-0"

Foyer

Dining Rm.
15'-0" x 12'-0"

Porch
8'-0" deep

FIRST FLOOR

Bedroom
12'-8" x 11'-4"

Bedroom
12'-10" x 12'-6"

Master Bedroom
15'-4" x 11'-0"

SECOND FLOOR

plan# HPK2800012

First Floor: 702 sq. ft.
Second Floor: 396 sq. ft.
Total: 1,098 sq. ft.
Bedrooms: 3
Bathrooms: 2
Width: 26' - 0"
Depth: 40' - 0"
Foundation: Crawlspace

ORDER ONLINE @ EPLANS.COM

This quaint country home with outside pillars and a front porch is chock full of living space. It's hard to believe that this modest-sized plan holds three bedrooms with walk-in closets, two baths, and a laundry. This is in addition to an open area that contains a farm-sized kitchen, a sunlit dining space, and a great room with a vaulted ceiling and fireplace. A rear deck, entered from the dining room, helps extend the living space to the outdoors.

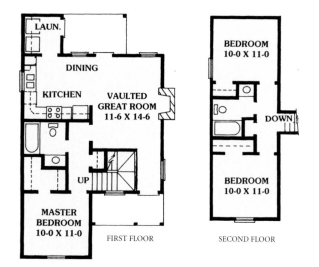

FIRST FLOOR

SECOND FLOOR

A lovely gazebo adorns the front porch of this one-story country home. It complements the other perfect details that distinguish this home from others of its size and configuration. On the inside, the living areas are clustered to the right of the plan: the great room with a fireplace, the sunny breakfast nook, and the kitchen with a peninsular work area. The master bedroom sits to the front of the plan and contains a walk-in closet and a bath with a separate tub and shower, two sinks, and a compartmented toilet.

plan# HPK2800013

Square Footage: 1,660
Bedrooms: 3
Bathrooms: 2
Width: 46' - 0"
Depth: 75' - 0"
Foundation: Crawlspace

ORDER ONLINE @ EPLANS.COM

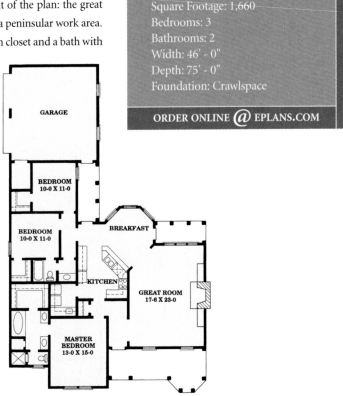

HELPFUL HINT! Typical home construction requires 8 to 12 copies of your plan.

plan# HPK2800014

First Floor: 772 sq. ft.
Second Floor: 411 sq. ft.
Total: 1,183 sq. ft.
Bedrooms: 2
Bathrooms: 2
Width: 32' - 0"
Depth: 28' - 7"
Foundation: Crawlspace

ORDER ONLINE @ EPLANS.COM

Perfect for a lakeside, vacation, or starter home, this two-story design with Victorian details is sure to be a favorite. A large covered porch is available for watching sunsets, and inside, the spacious living room sits conveniently close to the kitchen and dining area. A bedroom and a full hall bath finish off the first floor. Upstairs, a second bedroom, the laundry area, and a full bath round out the plan.

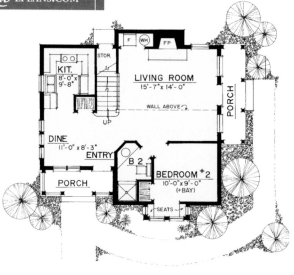

FIRST FLOOR

SECOND FLOOR

FIRST FLOOR

SECOND FLOOR

FIRST FLOOR

SECOND FLOOR

Options abound in this three-bedroom home. There is an optional two-car garage, which you may or may not build. The bonus room, which sits over the garage, may be finished at the initial building stages or left for future development. Living spaces on the first floor are comfortable and roomy. The great room enjoys both a warming gas fireplace and a built-in media center. The kitchen features a bayed breakfast nook. Two family bedrooms and a master suite reside on the second floor.

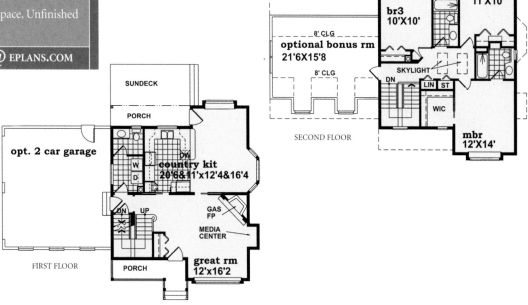

This compact traditional home offers an attractive exterior and a comfortable floor plan. The front door opens directly to the family room, which includes a fireplace and a built-in entertainment center. Just beyond, the kitchen features a walk-in pantry and adjoins a sunlit dining bay with access to the backyard. A two-car garage completes the first floor. Upstairs, three bedrooms are conveniently close to the laundry area. The master suite and Bedroom 2 provide walk-in closets.

plan# HPK2800018

First Floor: 716 sq. ft.
Second Floor: 754 sq. ft.
Total: 1,470 sq. ft.
Bedrooms: 3
Bathrooms: 2½
Width: 45' - 4"
Depth: 38' - 0"

ORDER ONLINE @ EPLANS.COM

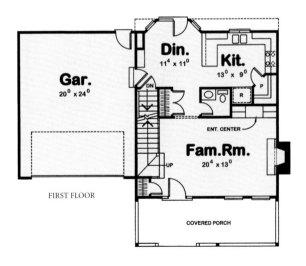

FIRST FLOOR

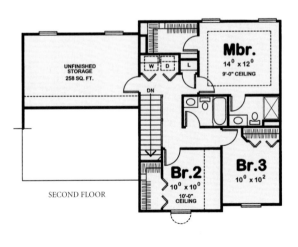

SECOND FLOOR

plan# HPK2800019

First Floor: 891 sq. ft.
Second Floor: 759 sq. ft.
Total: 1,650 sq. ft.
Bedrooms: 3
Bathrooms: 2½
Width: 44' - 0"
Depth: 40' - 0"

ORDER ONLINE @ EPLANS.COM

This modestly sized home provides a quaint covered front porch that opens to a two-story foyer. The formal dining room features a boxed window that can be seen from the entry. A fireplace in the great room adds warmth and coziness to the attached breakfast room and the well-planned kitchen. A powder room is nearby for guests. Three bedrooms occupy the second floor; one of these includes an arched window under a vaulted ceiling. The deluxe master suite provides a large walk-in closet and a dressing area with a double vanity and a whirlpool tub.

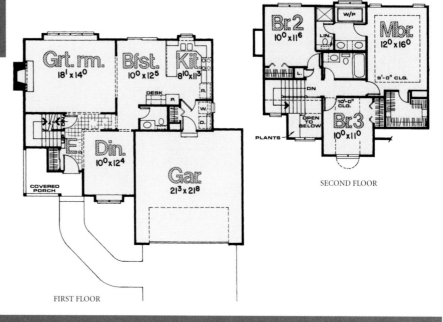

SECOND FLOOR

FIRST FLOOR

Established tradition meets new style with this country exterior—an old-fashioned covered porch complements sunbursts and asymmetrical gables. The tiled entry leads to a formal dining room or parlor and to casual living space, which includes a centered fireplace and views through three windows to the rear property. An L-shaped kitchen offers a snack bar, wide wrapping counters and a breakfast area with doors to the patio. A second-floor master suite hosts a roomy walk-in closet, windowed whirlpool tub, compartmented toilet and double-bowl vanity. A nearby secondary bedroom, with a window seat and an ample wardrobe, could be used as a study. Two additional bedrooms share a full bath.

plan# HPK2800020

First Floor: 866 sq. ft.
Second Floor: 905 sq. ft.
Total: 1,771 sq. ft.
Bedrooms: 4
Bathrooms: 2½
Width: 39' - 4"
Depth: 46' - 0"

ORDER ONLINE @ EPLANS.COM

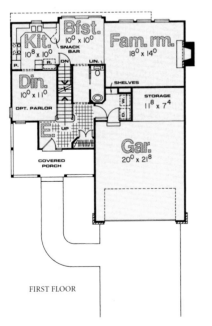

FIRST FLOOR

SECOND FLOOR

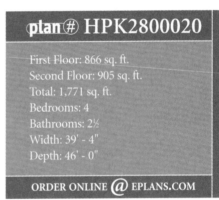

plan# HPK2800021

First Floor: 905 sq. ft.
Second Floor: 863 sq. ft.
Total: 1,768 sq. ft.
Bedrooms: 3
Bathrooms: 2½
Width: 40' - 8"
Depth: 46' - 0"

ORDER ONLINE @ EPLANS.COM

Multiple gables and different window treatments create an interesting exterior on this plan. A covered porch and Victorian accents create a classical elevation. Double doors to the entry open to a spacious great room and an elegant dining room. In the gourmet kitchen, features include an island snack bar and a large pantry—French doors lead to the breakfast area. Cathedral ceilings in the master suite and dressing area add an exquisite touch. A vaulted ceiling in Bedroom 2 accents a window seat and an arched transom window.

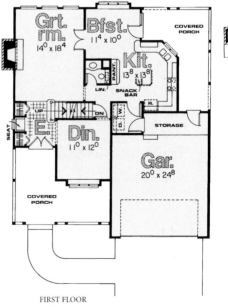

FIRST FLOOR

SECOND FLOOR

This home is distinguished by its two prominent dormers—one facing front and the other on the left side. The dormer to the left boasts a sunburst window that spills light into the family room. Enter through a large covered porch to a foyer that looks into the family room. Beyond, a vaulted kitchen/nook area is graced with an abundance of windows and rear-door access. The master bedroom is located at the front of the plan and is accented with a full bath. On the second floor are two additional bedrooms, each with ample closet space.

plan# HPK2800023

First Floor: 820 sq. ft.
Second Floor: 350 sq. ft.
Total: 1,170 sq. ft.
Bedrooms: 3
Bathrooms: 2
Width: 37' - 0"
Depth: 67' - 0"
Foundation: Slab

ORDER ONLINE @ EPLANS.COM

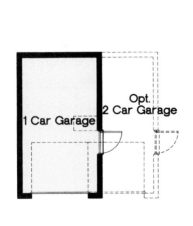

FIRST FLOOR

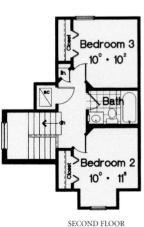

SECOND FLOOR

plan# HPK2800022

First Floor: 586 sq. ft.
Second Floor: 486 sq. ft.
Total: 1,072 sq. ft.
Bedrooms: 2
Bathrooms: 2½
Width: 40' - 0"
Depth: 40' - 0"
Foundation: Crawlspace

ORDER ONLINE @ EPLANS.COM

This quaint, country-style cottage would make a fine vacation retreat. Balusters and columns deck out the wraparound porch; the glass-paneled entry offers an elegant welcome. With a cozy fireplace and plenty of views in the great room, the interior is warmed by more than just heat—it enjoys a charming sense of the outdoors. The spacious great room provides an area for good conversation and plenty of relaxation. A well-organized kitchen has its own door to the wraparound porch. Upstairs, two bedrooms—each with a private bathroom—complete the plan.

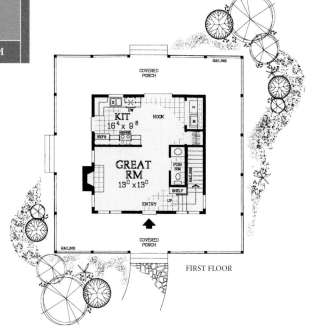

FIRST FLOOR

SECOND FLOOR

A country setting would be enhanced by this wonderful two-story home. Take advantage of the wraparound porch throughout the year for dining, relaxing, and entertaining. An open floor plan offers a functional layout. A great room sports a fireplace and views of the back yard. The spacious breakfast room provides access to the porch and is a great spot for entertaining friends who want to be near the cook. A U-shaped kitchen features a snack bar for quick bites. The first-floor master suite sits to the left of the plan. Upstairs, two secondary bedrooms make room for built-in bookcases and window seats. A full bath sits between the rooms.

plan# HPK2800024

First Floor: 1,086 sq. ft.
Second Floor: 554 sq. ft.
Total: 1,640 sq. ft.
Bedrooms: 3
Bathrooms: 2
Width: 52' - 0"
Depth: 43' - 0"
Foundation: Crawlspace

ORDER ONLINE @ EPLANS.COM

FIRST FLOOR

MASTER BEDRM 11⁸ x 13⁸
GREAT RM 15⁰ x 18⁸
NOOK 12⁰ x 12²
KIT 11⁸ x 10¹⁰
FOYER
MASTER BATH
WALK-IN CLOSET
COVERED PORCH
RAILING
SNACK BAR
LINE OF FLOOR ABOVE
SEAT

SECOND FLOOR

BEDRM 11⁸ x 12² + DORMER
BEDRM 11⁸ x 12² + DORMER
OPEN TO GREAT ROOM BELOW
ATTIC ACCESS
BATH
BUILT-IN DRESSER
SEAT STORAGE
RAILING
SEAT

HELPFUL HINT! Want an upgrade? Exchange your first purchase for a credit on a higher-priced plan within 90 days of ordering.

plan # HPK2800025

First Floor: 576 sq. ft.
Second Floor: 489 sq. ft.
Total: 1,065 sq. ft.
Bedrooms: 1
Bathrooms: 1½
Width: 24' - 0"
Depth: 31' - 0"
Foundation: Crawlspace

ORDER ONLINE @ EPLANS.COM

The steep rooflines on this home offer a sophisticated look that draws attention. Three dormers flood the home with light. The covered porch adds detailing to the posts. The entry leads to the two-story living room complete with a fireplace. The dining room is quite spacious and contains convenient access to the kitchen where a pantry room and plenty of counter space make cooking a treat in this home. The stairs to the second floor wrap around the fireplace and take the homeowners to the master bedroom and loft area.

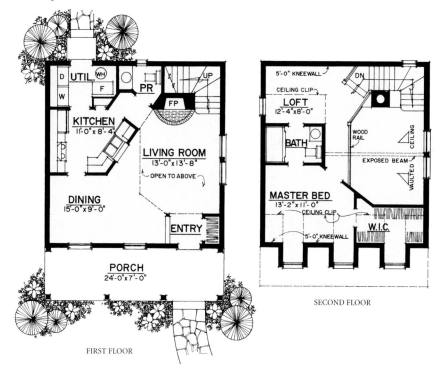

FIRST FLOOR

SECOND FLOOR

©1991 Donald A. Gardner, Inc.

This compact design has all the amenities available in larger plans with little wasted space. In addition, a wraparound covered porch, a front Palladian window, dormers, and rear arched windows provide exciting visual elements to the exterior. The spacious great room has a fireplace, a cathedral ceiling, and clerestory windows. A second-level balcony overlooks this gathering area. The kitchen is centrally located for maximum flexibility in layout and features a pass-through to the great room. Besides the generous master suite with a pampering bath, two family bedrooms located on the second level share a full bath.

plan # HPK2800026

First Floor: 1,325 sq. ft.
Second Floor: 453 sq. ft.
Total: 1,778 sq. ft.
Bedrooms: 3
Bathrooms: 2½
Width: 48' - 4"
Depth: 51' - 10"

ORDER ONLINE @ EPLANS.COM

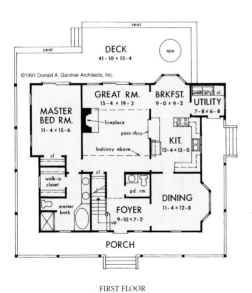

FIRST FLOOR

SECOND FLOOR

REAR EXTERIOR

plan# HPK2800028

Square Footage: 1,711
Bonus Space: 293 sq. ft.
Bedrooms: 3
Bathrooms: 2
Width: 61' - 0"
Depth: 50' - 0"

ORDER ONLINE @ EPLANS.COM

plan# HPK2800029

Square Footage: 1,677
Bonus Space: 355 sq. ft.
Bedrooms: 3
Bathrooms: 2
Width: 64' - 4"
Depth: 49' - 10"

ORDER ONLINE @ EPLANS.COM

plan# HPK2800030

Square Footage: 1,608
Bonus Space: 437 sq. ft.
Bedrooms: 3
Bathrooms: 2
Width: 40' - 8"
Depth: 62' - 8"

ORDER ONLINE @ EPLANS.COM

plan# HPK2800031

Square Footage: 1,307
Bedrooms: 3
Bathrooms: 2
Width: 40' - 0"
Depth: 61' - 10"

ORDER ONLINE @ EPLANS.COM

plan# HPK2800032

Square Footage: 1,643
Bonus Space: 338 sq. ft.
Bedrooms: 3
Bathrooms: 2
Width: 50' - 4"
Depth: 58' - 6"

ORDER ONLINE @ EPLANS.COM

Innovative and charming, this design features wonderful architectural detail and custom-styled features for its modest square footage. Topping a nostalgic front porch with columns, a large gable is enhanced with a decorative wooden bracket and half-circle window, and a metal roof accents a box-bay window that lies underneath an additional gable. Inside, flexibility abounds with a versatile study/bedroom and a bonus room above the garage. The kitchen—with an angled counter—separates a bright bay breakfast nook from the dining room that's crowned with a tray ceiling. An impressive rear dormer caps French doors to flood the great room with light, and built-in cabinetry and a striking fireplace make the great room even more enjoyable.

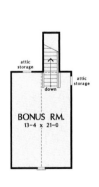

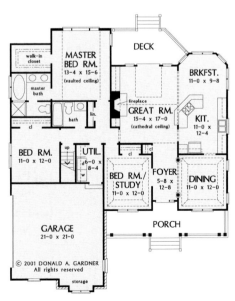

HELPFUL HINT! | Unlike plans from some other companies, each of our plans includes a full electrical schematic.

© 2003 Donald A. Gardner, Inc.

A welcoming front porch with bold columns and gables with decorative brackets add exciting curb appeal to this home. A sidelight and elliptical transom usher natural light into the foyer, and the open floor plan creates family efficiency. A single column and tray ceiling distinguishes the dining room without enclosing space. The kitchen connects to the dining room and is separated from the great room and breakfast nook by an angled counter. A built-in cabinet is positioned next to the fireplace and may conveniently hold media equipment. Featuring a cathedral ceiling, walk-in closet, and private bath, the master suite also has French doors that lead to the rear porch.

plan# HPK2800033

Square Footage: 1,660
Bonus Space: 374 sq. ft.
Bedrooms: 3
Bathrooms: 2
Width: 65' - 4"
Depth: 48' - 8"

ORDER ONLINE @ EPLANS.COM

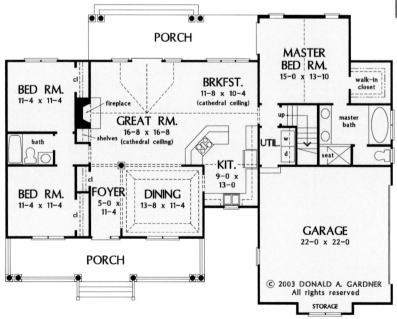

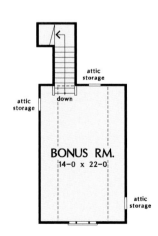

© 2003 Donald A. Gardner, Inc.

plan# HPK2800034

Square Footage: 1,727
Bonus Space: 346 sq. ft.
Bedrooms: 3
Bathrooms: 2
Width: 46' - 0"
Depth: 66' - 4"

ORDER ONLINE @ EPLANS.COM

This home offers both traditionally defined rooms and the flexibility of an open floor plan. A bay window and French doors invite light inside, and front and screened porches extend living space outdoors. With a breakfast counter, the kitchen is the heart of the home. A fireplace flanked by high windows enhances the great room, but can also be enjoyed from the kitchen. Tray ceilings crown the dining room, master bedroom, and study/bedroom; double doors leading into the study/bedroom add sophistication. The bonus room is perfectly positioned to create an additional bedroom, home gym, or playroom for the kids.

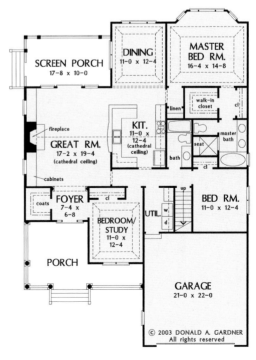

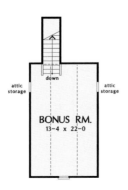

© 1997 Donald A. Gardner Architects, Inc.

The foyer opens to a spacious great room with a fireplace and a cathedral ceiling in this lovely traditional home. Sliding doors open to a rear deck from the great room, posing a warm welcome to enjoy the outdoors. The U-shaped kitchen features an angled peninsula counter with a cooktop. A private hall leads to the family sleeping quarters, which includes two bedrooms and a full bath with a double-bowl lavatory. Sizable bonus space above the garage provides a skylight.

plan# HPK2800027

Square Footage: 1,517
Bonus Space: 287 sq. ft.
Bedrooms: 3
Bathrooms: 2
Width: 61' - 4"
Depth: 48' - 6"

ORDER ONLINE @ EPLANS.COM

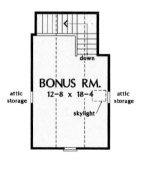

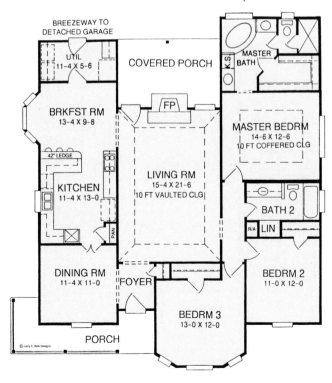

plan# HPK2800035

Square Footage: 1,772
Bedrooms: 3
Bathrooms: 2
Width: 45' - 8"
Depth: 50' - 2"
Foundation: Crawlspace, Slab

ORDER ONLINE @ EPLANS.COM

A folk Victorian flair gives this home its curb appeal. Inside, a large living room boasts a centerpiece fireplace and a coffered ceiling. The kitchen has a 42-inch-high breakfast bar and a pantry. The master suite includes a 10-foot coffered ceiling and a luxury bath with a corner whirlpool tub, separate shower, His and Hers vanities, and a roomy walk-in closet. Two additional bedrooms and a bath are nearby. A two-car garage plan is included with this design and can be connected to the home with a breezeway.

This absolutely charming Victorian-style ranch home is warm and inviting, yet the interior is decidedly up-to-date. An assemblage of beautiful windows surrounds the main entry, flooding the entrance foyer and adjoining great room with an abundance of shaded light. An elegant 10-foot stepped ceiling is featured in the great room, as is a corner fireplace and rear wall of French-style sliding doors. The beautiful multisided breakfast room features a 16-foot ceiling adorned with high clerestory windows, which become the exterior "turret." A private master suite includes a compartmented bath, dressing alcove, very large walk-in closet, 10-foot stepped ceiling, and beautiful bay window overlooking the backyard.

plan# HPK2800036

Square Footage: 1,466
Bedrooms: 3
Bathrooms: 2
Width: 60' - 0"
Depth: 39' - 10"
Foundation: Crawlspace, Slab, Unfinished Basement

ORDER ONLINE @ EPLANS.COM

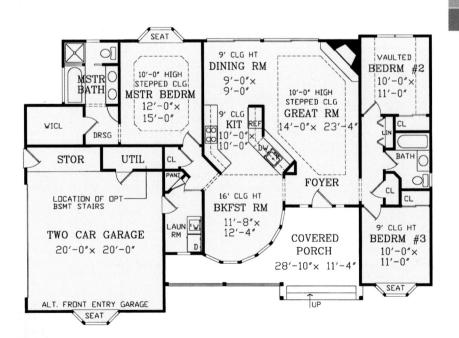

HELPFUL HINT! Our custom modification service can add a walk-out basement to any plan—great for hillside lots!

HOME FROM 1,800 TO 2,499 SQUARE FEET

Victorian homes may come in select shapes, but they're available in a wide range of sizes. A mid-sized Victorian is perfect for growing families or empty-nesters who want to scale down but retain a little extra room for visiting children and grand-kids. There are several advantages to living in a 1,800- to 2,499-square-foot home, namely the number of rooms. Not only do these homes usually include a third—or even fourth—bedroom, they also have dedicated rooms for entertaining often omitted in smaller designs, which makes them excellent for gatherings with family and friends.

The homes in the first section of this book are all about efficiency of space; the homes here have a little more elbow room. Dining rooms that previously doubled as more casual breakfast rooms have their own place, usually at the front of the home, and can be reserved for special occasions and meals. Formal living rooms can display fine furnishings, artwork, and collections, leaving the hearth-warmed family or recreation room to handle heavier traffic and use. With all of these new rooms occupying the first floor, bedrooms are bumped up to a second level where there's more space for extra bathrooms and more privacy. Greater square footage also pampers the homeowners with larger master suites: walk-in closets, double-vanity sinks, separate tubs and showers, and compartmented toilets complete the design. Even utility spaces feel the effects of more square feet with spacious laundry rooms and the addition of mudrooms and pantries.

Different stages of life demand different home accommodations. Whether you're preparing to move up or ready to take a step back, the homes in this section will provide you with myriad options to suit your situation, whatever it may be.

A signature Victorian porch, featuring a gazebo, creates a neighborly welcome. See more of plan HPK2800092 on page 90.

Victorian country style never looked so good! Turrets and carousel bays adorn the facade and create charming, comfortable living spaces inside, as bright windows flood the home with natural light. Enter from a wraparound covered porch to the two-story foyer. On the right, a wet bar complements the vaulted living room. Continue into the elegant dining room and gourmet kitchen with an island cooktop. The sunken family room is inviting and offers French doors to the rear property. A den at the front of the home makes an ideal guest room. Upstairs, the master suite achieves country glamour with a turret sitting area, lavish bath, and oversized walk-in closet. Two additional bedrooms share a full bath to complete the plan.

plan # HPK2800037

First Floor: 1,499 sq. ft.
Second Floor: 956 sq. ft.
Total: 2,455 sq. ft.
Bedrooms: 4
Bathrooms: 3
Width: 69' - 2"
Depth: 47' - 6"
Foundation: Crawlspace, Slab,
Unfinished Basement

ORDER ONLINE @ EPLANS.COM

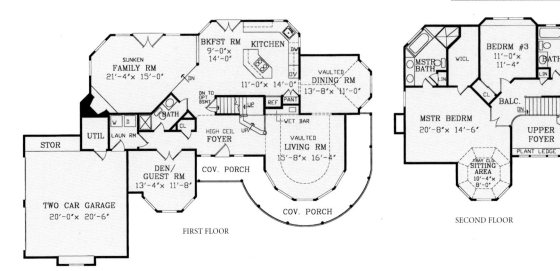

FIRST FLOOR

SECOND FLOOR

plan# HPK2800038

First Floor: 1,054 sq. ft.
Second Floor: 1,262 sq. ft.
Total: 2,316 sq. ft.
Bedrooms: 4
Bathrooms: 2½
Width: 54' - 0"
Depth: 34' - 8"

ORDER ONLINE @ EPLANS.COM

A two-story bay, a turret, and a wraparound porch create an eye-catching Victorian exterior. Inside, the parlor and the dining room are ideally situated for easy entertaining. Family and guests will delight in the gathering room, with its fireplace and built-in bookcases. The breakfast room offers sliding glass doors to the backyard as well as a pantry, a desk, and a nearby powder room. Upstairs, the skylit master suite pampers with a walk-in closet, a whirlpool tub, and dual sinks. Three family bedrooms share a large bath and a hall linen closet. Laundry facilities are also on this level.

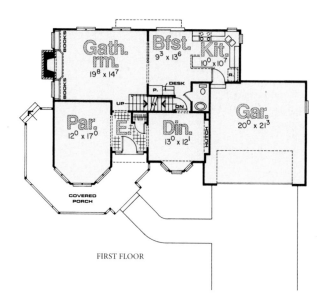

FIRST FLOOR

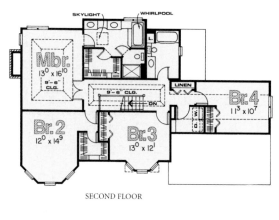

SECOND FLOOR

Victorian embellishments give a time-honored elegance to this classic family plan. Left of the entry, the front parlor opens to reveal a dramatic bay window. The formal dining room is large enough for a grand party and has easy access to the kitchen. Casual living is sure to center around the corner kitchen with a prep island and the adjoining breakfast room as they flow into the spacious family room. A split stair leads to the second floor, where an oversized master suite is accompanied by three family bedrooms and a full hall bath.

plan# HPK2800039

First Floor: 1,134 sq. ft.
Second Floor: 1,149 sq. ft.
Total: 2,283 sq. ft.
Bedrooms: 4
Bathrooms: 2½
Width: 53' - 4"
Depth: 42' - 0"

ORDER ONLINE @ EPLANS.COM

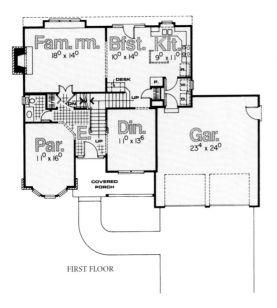

FIRST FLOOR

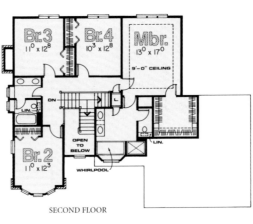

SECOND FLOOR

plan# HPK2800040

First Floor: 1,081 sq. ft.
Second Floor: 1,136 sq. ft.
Total: 2,217 sq. ft.
Bedrooms: 4
Bathrooms: 2½
Width: 53' - 0"
Depth: 42' - 0"

ORDER ONLINE @ EPLANS.COM

Victorian charm and detailing radiate from this design. Inside, formal living spaces begin with a dining room with hutch space and a parlor highlighted by a bay window. The T-shaped staircase allows quick access to the informal spaces at the rear, such as the comfortable gathering room with a fireplace, built-in bookcase, and many windows. Upstairs, a compartmented bath is shared by the secondary sleeping quarters. Gracing the master sleeping quarters is a private dressing/bath area offering an oval whirlpool tub, angled vanity, and walk-in wardrobe.

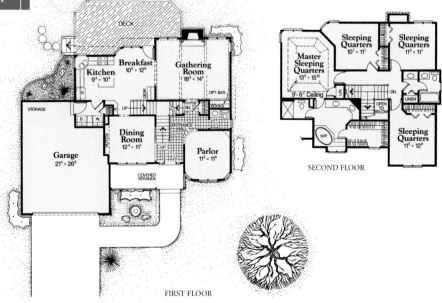

SECOND FLOOR

FIRST FLOOR

Beautiful arches and elaborate detail give the exterior of this four-bedroom home an unmistakable elegance. Inside, the floor plan is equally appealing. Note the formal dining room with a bay window, visible from the entrance hall. The large great room has a fireplace and a wall of windows with views of the rear property. A hearth room with a built-in bookcase adjoins the kitchen, which boasts a corner walk-in pantry and a spacious breakfast nook with a bay window. The first-floor master suite features His and Hers wardrobes and a large whirlpool tub.

plan # HPK2800041

First Floor: 1,653 sq. ft.
Second Floor: 700 sq. ft.
Total: 2,353 sq. ft.
Bedrooms: 4
Bathrooms: 2½
Width: 54' - 0"
Depth: 50' - 0"

ORDER ONLINE @ EPLANS.COM

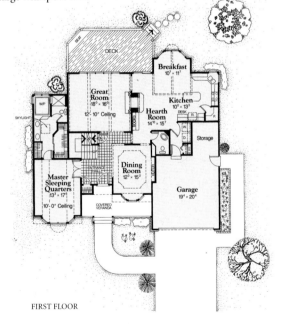

FIRST FLOOR

SECOND FLOOR

HELPFUL HINT! It is illegal to make copies of any plan except a "reproducible" version.

plan # HPK2800042

First Floor: 1,113 sq. ft.
Second Floor: 965 sq. ft.
Total: 2,078 sq. ft.
Bedrooms: 4
Bathrooms: 2½
Width: 46' - 0"
Depth: 41' - 5"

ORDER ONLINE @ EPLANS.COM

Elegant details make a pleasing facade on this four-bedroom, two-story Victorian home. From the large, bayed parlor with sloped ceiling to the sunken gathering room with fireplace, there's plenty to appreciate about the floor plan. The formal dining room opens to the parlor for convenient entertaining. An L-shaped kitchen with an attached breakfast room is nearby. Upstairs quarters include a master suite with a private dressing area and whirlpool bath, and three family bedrooms.

FIRST FLOOR

SECOND FLOOR

Farmhouse style is updated and improved on this home by a high roofline and a central arched window. The formal dining room with hutch space is conveniently located near the island kitchen. A main-floor laundry room with a sink is discreetly located next to the bright breakfast area with a desk and pantry. Highlighting the spacious great room are a raised-hearth fireplace, a cathedral ceiling, and trapezoid windows. Special features in the master suite include a large dressing area with a double vanity, skylight, step-up corner whirlpool tub, and generous walk-in closet. Upstairs, the three secondary bedrooms are separated from the master bedroom and share a hall bath.

plan# HPK2800043

First Floor: 1,505 sq. ft.
Second Floor: 610 sq. ft.
Total: 2,115 sq. ft.
Bedrooms: 4
Bathrooms: 2½
Width: 64' - 0"
Depth: 52' - 0"

ORDER ONLINE @ EPLANS.COM

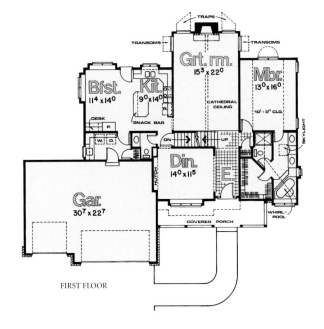

FIRST FLOOR

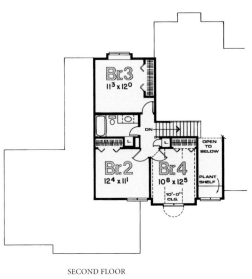

SECOND FLOOR

plan# HPK2800044

First Floor: 1,437 sq. ft.
Second Floor: 796 sq. ft.
Total: 2,233 sq. ft.
Bonus Space: 216 sq. ft.
Bedrooms: 4
Bathrooms: 3½
Width: 67' - 0"
Depth: 60' - 0"
Foundation: Crawlspace, Slab

ORDER ONLINE @ EPLANS.COM

The covered porch welcomes every guest and household member to a well-thought-out floor plan. The living room includes a fireplace and is open to a piano niche. The kitchen acts as a passage from the bayed dining room and sunny breakfast area. Privately located on the first floor, the master bedroom features a deluxe bath with a large walk-in closet. The second floor holds three family bedrooms and two baths. Note the private bath and bay window in Bedroom 2—great for a guest suite. Future expansion is available over the garage.

FIRST FLOOR

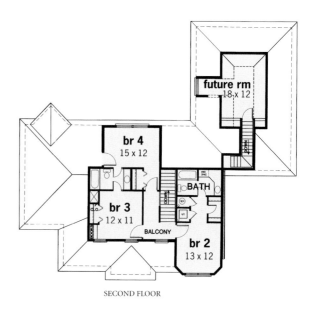

SECOND FLOOR

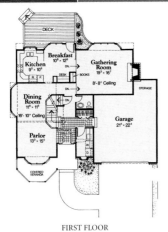

FIRST FLOOR

SECOND FLOOR

plan # HPK2800045

First Floor: 1,202 sq. ft.
Second Floor: 1,049 sq. ft.
Total: 2,251 sq. ft.
Bedrooms: 4
Bathrooms: 2½
Width: 50' - 0"
Depth: 40' - 0"

ORDER ONLINE @ EPLANS.COM

plan # HPK2800047

First Floor: 1,308 sq. ft.
Second Floor: 1,107 sq. ft.
Total: 2,415 sq. ft.
Bedrooms: 4
Bathrooms: 2½
Width: 54' - 0"
Depth: 42' - 0"

ORDER ONLINE @ EPLANS.COM

plan# HPK2800046

First Floor: 1,553 sq. ft.
Second Floor: 725 sq. ft.
Total: 2,278 sq. ft.
Bedrooms: 4
Bathrooms: 2½
Width: 54' - 0"
Depth: 50' - 0"

ORDER ONLINE @ EPLANS.COM

The intricate detailing, tall brick chimney, and stately veranda on the elevation of this four-bedroom, 1½-story home blend effortlessly into Victorian elegance. Other preferred features include the two-story entrance hall, a bay window in the formal dining room, the open island kitchen with a pantry and desk, the private master suite with a vaulted ceiling, and the two-person whirlpool tub in the master bath. This versatile plan is designed for practical living, with guest rooms or children's bedrooms located on the upper level. One of these second-story bedrooms features a walk-in closet.

SECOND FLOOR

FIRST FLOOR

HELPFUL HINT! All plans in this book were drawn by designers working under strict industry standards.

Fine details accentuate the heirloom dollhouse beauty of this narrow-lot Victorian home. Plenty of living space for get-togethers and scaled just right for solitary evenings, the dining room's twin set of French doors can be kept open to expand the space. An eat-in island kitchen makes room for casual meals and offers access to the rear deck. French doors also enhance the family room and provide front-porch access. Two secondary bedrooms share a compartmented bath and enjoy unique windows. The master suite is dressed up with a tray ceiling, French door access to the roomy bath, and a walk-in closet.

plan# HPK2800048

First Floor: 1,009 sq. ft.
Second Floor: 976 sq. ft.
Total: 1,985 sq. ft.
Bedrooms: 3
Bathrooms: 2½
Width: 31' - 2"
Depth: 42' - 0"
Foundation: Crawlspace, Unfinished Walkout Basement

ORDER ONLINE @ EPLANS.COM

DECK
30'-6" x 11'-7"

BRKFST

KITCHEN
15'-0" x 17'-0"

DINING
14'-8" x 12'-8"

UP

ENTRY
7'-11" x 15'-6"

FAMILY
18'-8" x 16'-0"

COATS

PORCH
30'-6" x 7'-7"

FIRST FLOOR

TRAY CEILING

MASTER BDRM
16'-4" x 15'-0"

D W

DN

BEDROOM 2
12'-0" x 12'-8"

BEDROOM 3
12'-8" x 12'-0"

WINDOW SEA

SECOND FLOOR

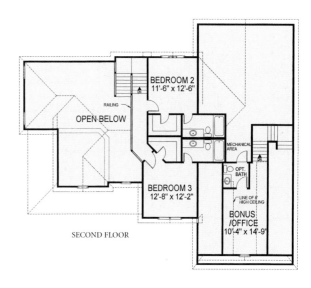

plan# HPK2800049

First Floor: 1,818 sq. ft.
Second Floor: 598 sq. ft.
Total: 2,416 sq. ft.
Bonus Space: 236 sq. ft.
Bedrooms: 3
Bathrooms: 3½
Width: 64' - 2"
Depth: 54' - 6"
Foundation: Crawlspace

ORDER ONLINE @ EPLANS.COM

This farmhouse design is truly extraordinary. Wood shingles, a window planter, and a brick veneer foundation accent the siding exterior. A wraparound porch makes this home irresistible. Flanking the foyer is the dining room on the right and the living room on the left, which features a vaulted ceiling and decorative columns crowned with a plant shelf. Just beyond is the family room that also offers vaulted ceilings plus built-in bookcases. The open kitchen provides abundant cabinets and a breakfast bar. The luxurious master suite boasts a tray ceiling, His and Hers closets, and a dramatic bath with a corner whirlpool tub. Upstairs, each of the secondary bedrooms feature a private bath and large walk-in closet. The bonus room/office makes this plan even more flexible.

With both farmhouse flavor and Victorian details, this plan features a wraparound veranda and a bayed area on the first and second floors as well as a turret on the second floor. Inside, the living room's many windows pour light in. The dining area begins with a bay window and is conveniently near the kitchen and breakfast area—also with a bay window. The U-shaped kitchen features an island workstation, ensuring plenty of space for cooking projects. A nearby lavatory is available for guests. The family room has an eye-catching corner-set fireplace. Upstairs, three family bedrooms share a full hall bath, while the master suite has a private bath and balcony, a large walk-in closet, and a sitting alcove, placed within the turret.

plan# HPK2800050

First Floor: 1,155 sq. ft.
Second Floor: 1,209 sq. ft.
Total: 2,364 sq. ft.
Bedrooms: 4
Bathrooms: 2½
Width: 46' - 0"
Depth: 36' - 8"
Foundation: Unfinished Basement

ORDER ONLINE @ EPLANS.COM

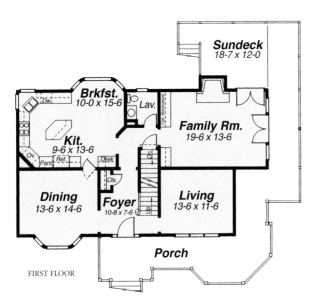

FIRST FLOOR

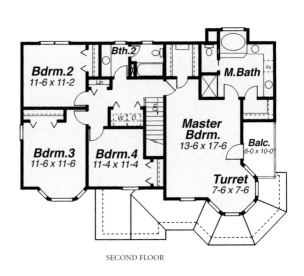

SECOND FLOOR

plan# HPK2800051

First Floor: 1,530 sq. ft.
Second Floor: 968 sq. ft.
Total: 2,498 sq. ft.
Bonus Space: 326 sq. ft.
Bedrooms: 3
Bathrooms: 2½
Width: 40' - 0"
Depth: 66' - 4"
Foundation: Crawlspace, Slab,
Unfinished Basement

ORDER ONLINE @ EPLANS.COM

The timeless influence of the French Quarter is exemplified in this home designed for riverfront living. The double French-door entry opens into a large living room/dining room area separated by a double archway. A railed balcony with a loft on the second floor overlooks the living room. A pass-through between the kitchen and dining room also provides seating at a bar for informal dining. The spacious master bedroom at the rear includes a sitting area and a roomy bath with a large walk-in closet. Two additional bedrooms, a bath, and a bonus area for an office or game room are located upstairs.

FIRST FLOOR

SECOND FLOOR

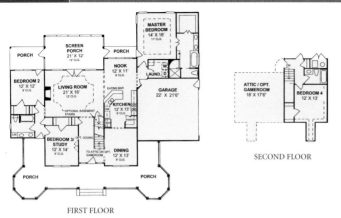

FIRST FLOOR

SECOND FLOOR

plan# HPK2800052

First Floor: 2,026 sq. ft.
Second Floor: 323 sq. ft.
Total: 2,349 sq. ft.
Bonus Space: 335 sq. ft.
Bedrooms: 4
Bathrooms: 3
Width: 69' - 0"
Depth: 65' - 6"

ORDER ONLINE @ EPLANS.COM

plan# HPK2800053

Square Footage: 2,485
Bedrooms: 3
Bathrooms: 2½
Width: 64' - 9"
Depth: 78' - 9"
Foundation: Finished Walkout
Basement

ORDER ONLINE @ EPLANS.COM

Helpful Hint!

A predrawn house plan is $8,000 to
$20,000 cheaper than a typical architect's
custom design.

© 1991 Donald A. Gardner Architects, Inc.

B. NATHAN.

plan# HPK2800054

Square Footage: 1,865
Bedrooms: 3
Bathrooms: 2
Width: 61' - 6"
Depth: 74' - 8"

ORDER ONLINE @ EPLANS.COM

This distinctive Victorian exterior conceals an open, contemporary floor plan. The entrance foyer with round columns offers visual excitement. The octagonal great room has a high tray ceiling and a fireplace. A generous kitchen with an angular island counter is centrally located, providing efficient service to the dining room, breakfast room, and deck. The luxurious master bedroom suite has a large walk-in closet and a compartmented bath. Two additional bedrooms—one that would make a lovely study by including an entrance off the foyer—and a full hall bath round out this favorite plan.

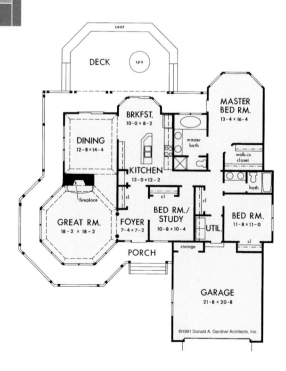

Gables accented with cedar shakes join with a shed dormer to create a charming cottage exterior. Arts and Crafts columns highlight arches on the front porch, and the front-entry garage provides convenience. Over the front door, a transom floods the foyer with natural light, and the absence of two walls in the dining room give the feeling of airiness to the common rooms. An angled counter, built-in cabinetry, and French doors add a custom-styled touch to the interior, providing both beauty and function. A rear porch encourages outdoor living, while a bonus room offers flexible space above the garage. The utility room/mudroom provides additional built-in shelving for storage.

plan# HPK2800055

Square Footage: 1,965
Bedrooms: 3
Bathrooms: 2
Width: 54' - 4"
Depth: 59' - 0"

ORDER ONLINE @ EPLANS.COM

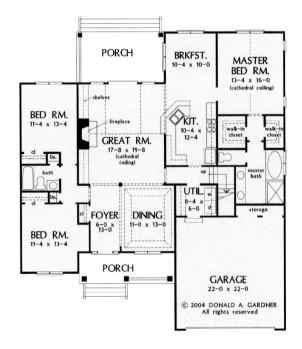

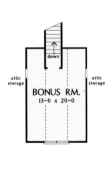

© 2004 Donald A. Gardner, Inc.

plan# HPK2800056

First Floor: 1,502 sq. ft.
Second Floor: 549 sq. ft.
Total: 2,051 sq. ft.
Bonus Space: 285 sq. ft.
Bedrooms: 3
Bathrooms: 2½
Width: 43' - 0"
Depth: 57' - 6"

ORDER ONLINE @ EPLANS.COM

A stone-and-siding exterior creates incredible curb appeal for this country cottage. Decorative brackets accent the gables, and a metal roof tops columns on the front and rear porches. Inside, the floor plan opens common areas—kitchen, great room, and breakfast area—to each other, and uses a balcony to divide the two-story foyer from the great room. A dining room near the front entry provides a formal atmosphere for meals. Bay windows extend the floor space here as well as in the breakfast nook and master bedroom. A tray ceiling, also in the master bedroom, creates height, while a conventional closet paired with a walk-in provides space for clothes and other storage. A corner shower and corner tub give the master bath spa-like luxury. Above the garage, a bonus room provides space for a family's everchanging needs, and a large linen closet adds space for storage.

FIRST FLOOR

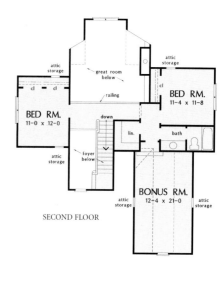

SECOND FLOOR

© 2002 Donald A. Gardner, Inc.

With a brick-and-siding exterior and beautiful box-bay windows, this home will complement any neighborhood. A fireplace and tray ceiling add a cozy element in the great room, and a window seat in the breakfast nook adds comfort and charm. The master suite is located on the far right, with dual walk-in closets and a fantastic bath. To the far left, three family bedrooms—or make one a study—all have outstanding features. Bonus space above the garage provides room to grow.

plan # HPK2800057

Square Footage: 2,076
Bonus Space: 351 sq. ft.
Bedrooms: 4
Bathrooms: 2
Width: 55' - 4"
Depth: 60' - 6"

ORDER ONLINE @ EPLANS.COM

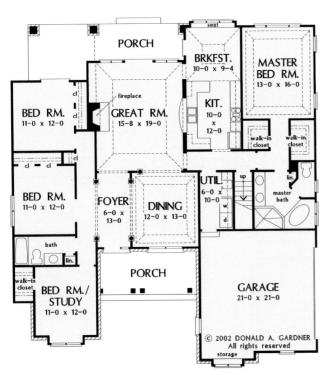

© 2003 Donald A. Gardner, Inc.

plan# HPK2800058

First Floor: 1,569 sq. ft.
Second Floor: 504 sq. ft.
Total: 2,073 sq. ft.
Bonus Space: 320 sq. ft.
Bedrooms: 3
Bathrooms: 2½
Width: 47' - 0"
Depth: 55' - 0"

ORDER ONLINE @ EPLANS.COM

Low-maintenance siding, a convenient front-entry garage, and architectural details such as gables and half-circle transoms make this narrow-lot charmer perfect for beginning families and empty-nesters. An abundance of windows and an open floor plan flood this home with natural light. Custom-styled features include a fireplace, two-story great room ceiling, kitchen pass-through, and French doors leading to the rear porch. The master suite is complete with a vaulted ceiling in the bedroom, walk-in and wardrobe closets, a double vanity, garden tub, and separate shower. Two secondary bedrooms share a full bath with the bonus room.

FIRST FLOOR

SECOND FLOOR

HELPFUL HINT! Bonus rooms generally are not calculated in the total square footage of a home.

© 1991 Donald A. Gardner Architects, Inc.

An extensive wraparound porch and a luxurious deck dramatically increase the living space of this quintessential farmhouse. The foyer opens to the master suite and a glorious two-story great room that offers stupendous views and a cozy fireplace. The kitchen with an island workspace serves the formal dining room and sunny breakfast nook. The master suite has a walk-in closet and bath with a double-bowl vanity, shower and garden tub. The second floor consists of three bedrooms: one has a private bath while the other two share a full bath.

plan# HPK2800059

First Floor: 1,519 sq. ft.
Second Floor: 792 sq. ft.
Total: 2,311 sq. ft.
Bedrooms: 4
Bathrooms: 3½
Width: 62' - 10"
Depth: 80' - 4"

ORDER ONLINE @ EPLANS.COM

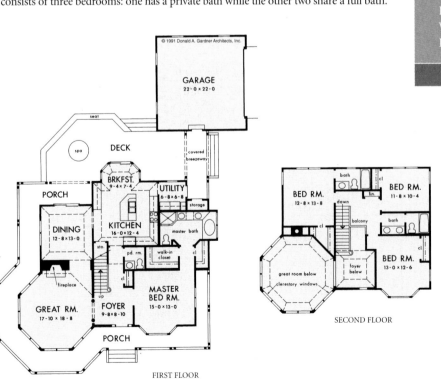

FIRST FLOOR

SECOND FLOOR

plan# HPK2800060

First Floor: 1,276 sq. ft.
Second Floor: 1,074 sq. ft.
Total: 2,350 sq. ft.
Bedrooms: 3
Bathrooms: 2½
Width: 43' - 0"
Depth: 51' - 10"

ORDER ONLINE @ EPLANS.COM

A turret, gables, and filigree accents add up to this Victorian charmer. Inside, the downstairs turret is an extension of the living room, while upstairs it belongs to the master bedroom and can be a study or sitting area. A special attraction in this home is the sunroom, which opens from the kitchen and extends out onto the rear deck. The dining room provides a box-bay window and access to the covered deck, which leads to a hot tub and a deck with built-in seats. The family room also accesses the deck. A powder room off the foyer, a utility room, and a covered breezeway with a garage option complete the first floor. Three bedrooms upstairs include the master suite, two bedrooms, and a shared bath that provides separate vanities.

SECOND FLOOR

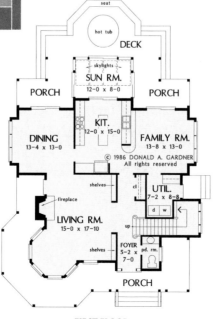

FIRST FLOOR

Covered porches front and back are a fine preview to the livable nature of this Victorian home. Living areas are defined in a family room with a fireplace, formal living and dining rooms, and a kitchen with a breakfast room. An ample laundry room, a garage with a storage area, and a powder room round out the first floor. Three second-floor bedrooms are joined by a study and two full baths. The master suite on this floor has two closets, including an ample walk-in, as well as a relaxing bath with a tile-rimmed whirlpool tub and a separate shower with a seat.

plan# HPK2800061

First Floor: 1,375 sq. ft.
Second Floor: 1,016 sq. ft.
Total: 2,391 sq. ft.
Bedrooms: 3
Bathrooms: 2½
Width: 62' - 7"
Depth: 54' - 0"
Foundation: Unfinished Basement

ORDER ONLINE @ EPLANS.COM

FIRST FLOOR

SECOND FLOOR

plan # HPK2800062

First Floor: 1,269 sq. ft.
Second Floor: 1,227 sq. ft.
Total: 2,496 sq. ft.
Bedrooms: 4
Bathrooms: 2½
Width: 70' - 0"
Depth: 44' - 5"
Foundation: Unfinished Basement

ORDER ONLINE @ EPLANS.COM

Sunbursts, simple balusters, and a stylish turret set off this Victorian exterior, complete with two finely detailed covered porches. An unrestrained floor plan offers bays and nooks, open spaces, and cozy niches—a proper combination for an active family. Formal living and dining areas invite gatherings, whether large or small, planned or casual—but the heart of the home is the family area. A wide bay window and a fireplace with an extended hearth warm up both the family room and breakfast area; the nearby kitchen offers a snack counter for easy meals. The second floor includes three family bedrooms and a lavish master suite with an oversized whirlpool spa and two walk-in closets.

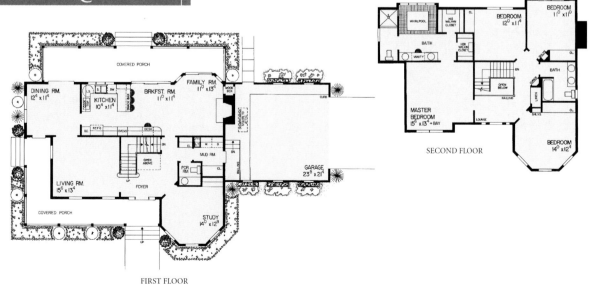

This Victorian-style exterior—a wraparound porch, mullion windows, and turret-style bays—offers a wonderful floor plan. Inside, an impressive tiled entry opens to the formal rooms, which nestle to the left side of the plan and enjoy natural light from an abundance of windows. More than just a pretty face, the turret houses a secluded study on the first level and provides a sunny bay window for a family bedroom upstairs. The second-level master suite boasts its own fireplace, a dressing area with a walk-in closet, and a lavish bath with a garden tub and twin vanities. The two-car garage offers space for a workshop or extra storage.

plan# HPK2800063

First Floor: 1,186 sq. ft.
Second Floor: 988 sq. ft.
Total: 2,174 sq. ft.
Bedrooms: 4
Bathrooms: 2½
Width: 72' - 4"
Depth: 51' - 2"
Foundation: Unfinished Basement

ORDER ONLINE @ EPLANS.COM

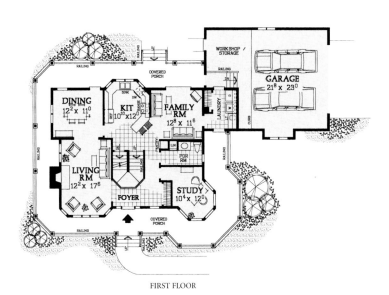

FIRST FLOOR

SECOND FLOOR

HELPFUL HINT! Rest easy: All of our home designs conform to national uniform building codes.

plan# HPK2800064

First Floor: 1,321 sq. ft.
Second Floor: 1,070 sq. ft.
Total: 2,391 sq. ft.
Bedrooms: 4
Bathrooms: 3
Width: 63' - 2"
Depth: 50' - 8"
Foundation: Crawlspace, Unfinished Basement

ORDER ONLINE @ EPLANS.COM

FIRST FLOOR

SECOND FLOOR

plan# HPK2800065

First Floor: 1,193 sq. ft.
Second Floor: 1,188 sq. ft.
Total: 2,381 sq. ft.
Bedrooms: 4
Bathrooms: 2½
Width: 62' - 0"
Depth: 47' - 0"
Foundation: Crawlspace, Unfinished Basement

ORDER ONLINE @ EPLANS.COM

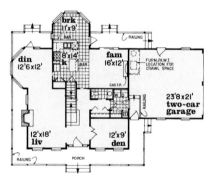

FIRST FLOOR

SECOND FLOOR

A gazebo porch, topped with a turret roof, and nostalgic wood detailing grace this four-bedroom Victorian design. Double front doors open to a spacious living room and adjoining dining room. The living room has a warming fireplace. The kitchen, with a center prep island and raised eating bar, serves a sunny breakfast bay and the family room. A door leads out to a rear patio. The family room shares the warmth of its hearth with the kitchen and breakfast bay. All four bedrooms are on the second floor. The master suite features a bay window, walk-in closet, and a bath with a corner whirlpool tub that's adorned by columns. Three family bedrooms share a full bath. A small study area is located at the top of the stairs.

plan# HPK2800066

First Floor: 1,128 sq. ft.
Second Floor: 1,130 sq. ft.
Total: 2,258 sq. ft.
Bedrooms: 4
Bathrooms: 2½
Width: 48' - 0"
Depth: 53' - 0"
Foundation: Crawlspace, Unfinished Basement

ORDER ONLINE @ EPLANS.COM

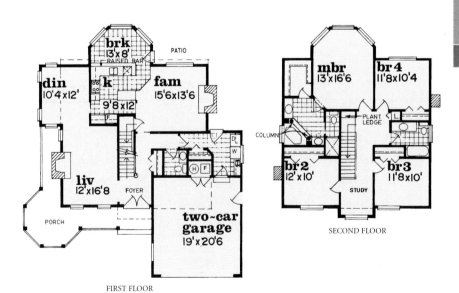

FIRST FLOOR

SECOND FLOOR

plan# HPK2800067

First Floor: 1,136 sq. ft.
Second Floor: 1,083 sq. ft.
Total: 2,219 sq. ft.
Bedrooms: 4
Bathrooms: 2½
Width: 25' - 6"
Depth: 54' - 9"
Foundation: Crawlspace, Unfinished Basement

ORDER ONLINE @ EPLANS.COM

This inviting narrow-lot design borrows classic details from a bygone era—a covered veranda in the front, a gabled roof, and fish-scale detailing. Ideal for city lots, this design features four bedrooms, including a master suite with a walk-in closet and a private bath that includes a separate tub and shower and double-bowl vanity. One of the family bedrooms is graced by a box window. First-floor living areas include a formal living room, with a gas fireplace, that opens to a dining room. Toward the rear of the home, a kitchen overlooks a breakfast nook and the family room, which is warmed by another gas fireplace.

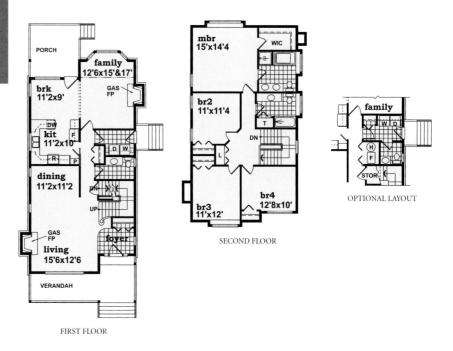

FIRST FLOOR

SECOND FLOOR

OPTIONAL LAYOUT

With details reminiscent of Victorian design, this home is graced by a covered veranda wrapping on three sides and an elegant bay window. The vaulted foyer introduces an octagonal staircase and an archway to the living room. Details in the living room include a tray ceiling and adjoining dining room with beamed ceiling. French doors in the dining room open to the porch. A country kitchen offers a spacious walk-in pantry, a center prep island, and a breakfast bay with porch access. The nearby family room has its own fireplace. The upstairs master bedroom is graced by a bayed sitting area and bath with private deck. Bedrooms 2, 3, and 4 share the use of a full hall bath. A railed gallery on the second floor overlooks the foyer below and is brightened by the bay windows.

plan# HPK2800068

First Floor: 1,205 sq. ft.
Second Floor: 1,254 sq. ft.
Total: 2,459 sq. ft.
Bedrooms: 4
Bathrooms: 2½
Width: 71' - 6"
Depth: 56' - 6"
Foundation: Crawlspace, Unfinished Basement

ORDER ONLINE @ EPLANS.COM

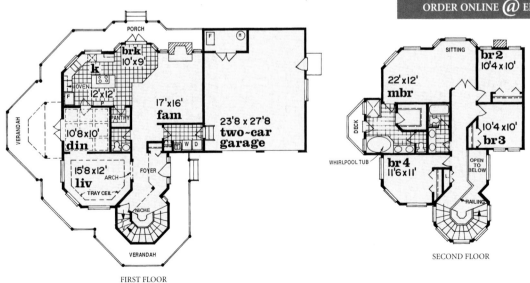

FIRST FLOOR

SECOND FLOOR

plan# HPK2800069

First Floor: 1,180 sq. ft.
Second Floor: 1,121 sq. ft.
Total: 2,301 sq. ft.
Bedrooms: 4
Bathrooms: 2½
Width: 48' - 0"
Depth: 52' - 6"
Foundation: Crawlspace, Unfinished Basement

ORDER ONLINE @ EPLANS.COM

A turret roof, prominent bay window, and wraparound veranda designate this four-bedroom design as classic Victorian. The plans include two second-level layouts—one with four bedrooms or one with three bedrooms and a vaulted ceiling over the family room. Both include a lavish master suite with an octagonal tray ceiling in the sitting room, a walk-in closet, and a private bath with a columned whirlpool spa and separate shower. The first floor holds a formal living room with windows overlooking the veranda, a formal dining room, and a family room with a fireplace. The U-shaped kitchen has a sunny breakfast bay. A half-bath and a laundry room are found in the service area that also leads to the two-car garage.

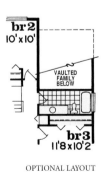

OPTIONAL LAYOUT

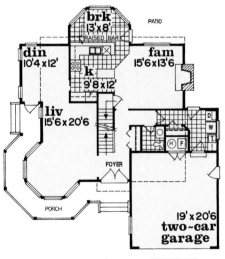

FIRST FLOOR

SECOND FLOOR

Special attention to exterior details and interior nuances gives this relaxed farmhouse fine distinction on any street. From the large covered porch, enter to find a spacious, thoughtful plan. A striking central staircase separates the first-floor living area, which boasts a home office and a cathedral ceiling in the living room. The second floor includes a master suite, two secondary bedrooms that share a full bath, and a flexible upstairs sitting area. The master suite contains a bath with a double-bowl vanity and a walk-in closet.

plan # HPK2800070

First Floor: 1,274 sq. ft.
Second Floor: 1,009 sq. ft.
Total: 2,283 sq. ft.
Bedrooms: 3
Bathrooms: 2½
Width: 50' - 0"
Depth: 46' - 0"
Foundation: Unfinished Basement

ORDER ONLINE @ EPLANS.COM

SECOND FLOOR

FIRST FLOOR

plan# HPK2800071

First Floor: 1,319 sq. ft.
Second Floor: 1,107 sq. ft.
Total: 2,426 sq. ft.
Bedrooms: 3
Bathrooms: 2½
Width: 52' - 0"
Depth: 46' - 8"
Foundation: Unfinished Basement

ORDER ONLINE @ EPLANS.COM

The traditional charm of this family home offers a distinct American flavor. Horizontal siding and a quaint wraparound front porch are sure signs of country styling. To the left of the foyer, the home office is a quiet retreat. To the right is a combined living and dining room area. The gourmet kitchen features a snack bar overlooking the rear porch and is open to a casual family area with a fireplace. A two-car garage, laundry room, and half-bath complete the first floor. Upstairs, the master suite offers a private bath and massive walk-in closet.

SECOND FLOOR

FIRST FLOOR

This charming country traditional home provides a well-lit home office, harbored in a beautiful bay with three windows. The second-floor bay brightens the master bath, which has a double-bowl vanity, a step-up tub, and a dressing area. The living and dining rooms share a two-sided fireplace. The gourmet kitchen has a cooktop island counter and enjoys outdoor views through sliding glass doors in the breakfast area. A sizable bonus room above the two-car garage can be developed into hobby space or a recreation room.

plan # HPK2800072

First Floor: 1,044 sq. ft.
Second Floor: 892 sq. ft.
Total: 1,936 sq. ft.
Bonus Space: 228 sq. ft.
Bedrooms: 3
Bathrooms: 2½
Width: 58' - 0"
Depth: 43' - 6"
Foundation: Unfinished Basement

ORDER ONLINE @ EPLANS.COM

FIRST FLOOR

SECOND FLOOR

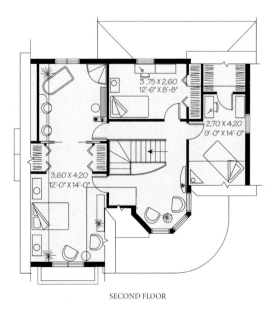

SECOND FLOOR

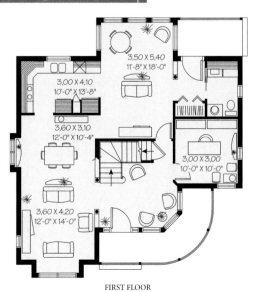

FIRST FLOOR

plan# HPK2800073

First Floor: 1,070 sq. ft.
Second Floor: 970 sq. ft.
Total: 2,040 sq. ft.
Bedrooms: 3
Bathrooms: 1½
Width: 36' - 0"
Depth: 40' - 8"
Foundation: Unfinished Basement

ORDER ONLINE @ EPLANS.COM

Victorian styling can come in an affordable size, as this home shows. A sitting area inside the front hall connects with the family room for handling large parties. An enclosed room off the sitting area can be used as a study or extra bedroom. A combination half-bath and laundry is just inside the rear entrance for quick cleanup; the covered rear porch is accessed from a door just beyond the laundry area. For easy upkeep, the three bedrooms on the second floor share a full bath that includes a corner tub. One of the bedrooms offers access to a private balcony.

FIRST FLOOR

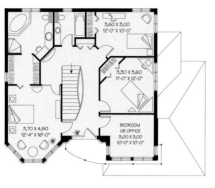

SECOND FLOOR

plan# HPK2800074

First Floor: 934 sq. ft.
Second Floor: 1,108 sq. ft.
Total: 2,042 sq. ft.
Bedrooms: 4
Bathrooms: 2½
Width: 44' - 8"
Depth: 36' - 0"
Foundation: Unfinished Basement

ORDER ONLINE @ EPLANS.COM

FIRST FLOOR

SECOND FLOOR

plan# HPK2800075

First Floor: 1,334 sq. ft.
Second Floor: 965 sq. ft.
Total: 2,299 sq. ft.
Bedrooms: 3
Bathrooms: 2
Width: 40' - 8"
Depth: 32' - 8"
Foundation: Unfinished Basement

ORDER ONLINE @ EPLANS.COM

Helpful Hint!

A home automation upgrade provides all
the wiring diagrams needed to build a
Smart House.

plan# HPK2800073

First Floor: 1,070 sq. ft.
Second Floor: 970 sq. ft.
Total: 2,040 sq. ft.
Bedrooms: 3
Bathrooms: 1½
Width: 36' - 0"
Depth: 40' - 8"
Foundation: Unfinished Basement

ORDER ONLINE @ EPLANS.COM

Victorian styling can come in an affordable size, as this home shows. A sitting area inside the front hall connects with the family room for handling large parties. An enclosed room off the sitting area can be used as a study or extra bedroom. A combination half-bath and laundry is just inside the rear entrance for quick cleanup; the covered rear porch is accessed from a door just beyond the laundry area. For easy upkeep, the three bedrooms on the second floor share a full bath that includes a corner tub. One of the bedrooms offers access to a private balcony.

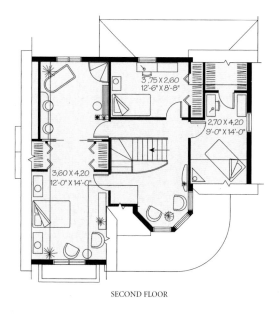

SECOND FLOOR

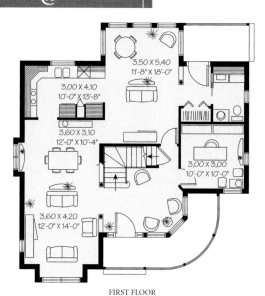

FIRST FLOOR

FIRST FLOOR

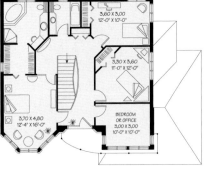

SECOND FLOOR

plan# HPK2800074

First Floor: 934 sq. ft.
Second Floor: 1,108 sq. ft.
Total: 2,042 sq. ft.
Bedrooms: 4
Bathrooms: 2 ½
Width: 44' - 8"
Depth: 36' - 0"
Foundation: Unfinished Basement

ORDER ONLINE @ EPLANS.COM

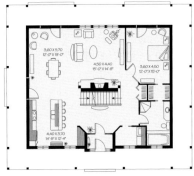

FIRST FLOOR

SECOND FLOOR

plan# HPK2800075

First Floor: 1,334 sq. ft.
Second Floor: 965 sq. ft.
Total: 2,299 sq. ft.
Bedrooms: 3
Bathrooms: 2
Width: 40' - 8"
Depth: 32' - 8"
Foundation: Unfinished Basement

ORDER ONLINE @ EPLANS.COM

Helpful Hint!

A home automation upgrade provides all the wiring diagrams needed to build a Smart House.

plan# HPK2800076

First Floor: 1,337 sq. ft.
Second Floor: 1,025 sq. ft.
Total: 2,362 sq. ft.
Bedrooms: 3
Bathrooms: 2½
Width: 50' - 6"
Depth: 72' - 6"
Foundation: Crawlspace

ORDER ONLINE @ EPLANS.COM

This Victorian design is far more than just a pretty face. The turret houses a spacious den with built-in cabinetry on the first floor and provides a sunny bay window for the family bedroom upstairs. Just off the foyer, the formal living and dining rooms create an elegant open space for entertaining, while a focal-point fireplace with an extended hearth warms up the spacious family area. The cooktop-island kitchen and morning nook lead to a powder room and laundry area. Two second-floor bedrooms share a full bath, while the master suite offers a private bath with an oversized whirlpool tub, twin vanities, and a walk-in closet.

FIRST FLOOR

SECOND FLOOR

GARAGE
21-4 x 21-8

LAUN.

DINING ROOM
12-0 x 12-0

GREAT ROOM
16-8 x 22-0

UP

GUEST
11-0 x 12-0

FIRST FLOOR

BEDROOM
11-6 x 12-0

MASTER BEDROOM
13-6 x 17-6

SITTING ROOM
8-8 x 16-8

BEDROOM
11-6 x 12-0

DN

SECOND FLOOR

plan # HPK2800077

First Floor: 1,274 sq. ft.
Second Floor: 1,178 sq. ft.
Total: 2,452 sq. ft.
Bedrooms: 4
Bathrooms: 3
Width: 30' - 0"
Depth: 80' - 0"
Foundation: Crawlspace

ORDER ONLINE @ EPLANS.COM

GARAGE
19-4 x 19-8

STORAGE

KEEPING ROOM
13-0 x 15-8

UP

BREAKFAST
8-0 x 12-4

DINING ROOM
10-10 x 12-0

FOYER

LIVING ROOM
15-0 X 17-0

FIRST FLOOR

BEDROOM
10-10 x 11-0

BEDROOM
10-4 x 11-10

BEDROOM
11-0 x 11-0

LAUN.

DOWN

MASTER BEDROOM
13-0 x 15-0

SECOND FLOOR

plan # HPK2800078

First Floor: 1,184 sq. ft.
Second Floor: 1,093 sq. ft.
Total: 2,277 sq. ft.
Bedrooms: 4
Bathrooms: 2½
Width: 28' - 0"
Depth: 74' - 0"
Foundation: Crawlspace

ORDER ONLINE @ EPLANS.COM

plan⊕ HPK2800079

First Floor: 1,105 sq. ft.
Second Floor: 979 sq. ft.
Total: 2,084 sq. ft.
Bedrooms: 3
Bathrooms: 2½
Width: 30' - 0"
Depth: 45' - 0"
Foundation: Crawlspace

ORDER ONLINE @ EPLANS.COM

A charming, historically informed exterior makes this narrow-lot plan perfect for traditional urban neighborhoods. Delicate Victorian detailing and materials further contribute to the home's streetside presence. Living spaces have been slightly updated to include a great room and open kitchen, but a formal living room and dining room still exist. A smart layout allows for continuous line of sight from the front bay window to the rear entry, enhancing the home's modest square footage. Upstairs, private rooms are comfortable and sunny. Note the oversized walk-in closet attending the master suite.

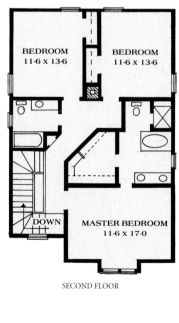

SECOND FLOOR

FIRST FLOOR

FIRST FLOOR

SECOND FLOOR

plan # HPK2800080

First Floor: 1,259 sq. ft.
Second Floor: 1,181 sq. ft.
Total: 2,440 sq. ft.
Bedrooms: 3
Bathrooms: 2½
Width: 44' - 0"
Depth: 46' - 0"
Foundation: Crawlspace

ORDER ONLINE @ EPLANS.COM

FIRST FLOOR

SECOND FLOOR

plan # HPK2800081

First Floor: 1,148 sq. ft.
Second Floor: 1,095 sq. ft.
Total: 2,243 sq. ft.
Bedrooms: 3
Bathrooms: 2½
Width: 42' - 0"
Depth: 42' - 0"
Foundation: Crawlspace

ORDER ONLINE @ EPLANS.COM

Here's an eye-catcher that will surely be unique in your neighborhood. It's a country home, but with lots of ornate trimmings—a row of spires across the top ridge, a decorative chimney, pedimented gables, and a clerestory window that draws sunlight into the foyer. Inside, all the living area is on the first floor and the sleeping space on the second. An open floor plan has the dining room to the right of the foyer and the great room with a large fireplace to the left. To the rear of these formal social areas is the center of family activity, a spacious keeping room with its own warming fireplace. It flows into the ample kitchen in one direction and out onto a deck from the other. Four bedrooms and three baths are located upstairs. The plan also comes with a detached garage.

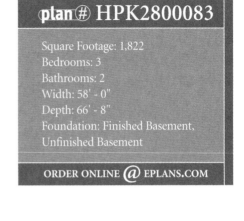

plan# HPK2800083

Square Footage: 1,822
Bedrooms: 3
Bathrooms: 2
Width: 58' - 0"
Depth: 66' - 8"
Foundation: Finished Basement,
Unfinished Basement

ORDER ONLINE @ EPLANS.COM

©The Sater Design Collection, Inc.

plan# HPK2800084

Square Footage: 1,848
Bedrooms: 3
Bathrooms: 2
Width: 58' - 0"
Depth: 59' - 6"
Foundation: Crawlspace

ORDER ONLINE @ EPLANS.COM

©The Sater Design Collection, Inc.

©The Sater Design Collection, Inc.

plan # HPK2800085

First Floor: 1,710 sq. ft.
Second Floor: 618 sq. ft.
Total: 2,328 sq. ft.
Bedrooms: 3
Bathrooms: 3
Width: 47' - 0"
Depth: 50' - 0"
Foundation: Crawlspace

ORDER ONLINE @ EPLANS.COM

Decorative details complement this home's country facade, and pedimented arches and a covered porch add sophistication. The foyer leads to the vaulted great room where a fireplace awaits. Both the magnificent master suite and the great room showcase French doors to the rear vaulted porch. The breakfast bay sheds sunlight onto the spacious kitchen. An elegant coffered ceiling and three-window bay dress up the front study (or make it into an office). Two bedrooms, both with walk-in closets, share the second level with a bath and an equipment room.

SECOND FLOOR

FIRST FLOOR

©The Sater Design Collection, Inc.

Matchstick trim and arch-top windows create plenty of curb appeal with this attractive design. A spacious leisure room with a stepped ceiling highlights the heart of the home. To the left of the plan, a rambling master suite boasts access to a private porch. The formal dining room adjoins the gourmet kitchen, which features a breakfast nook and a walk-in pantry. French doors lead out to the rear porch and an outdoor kitchen. The first-floor master suite features a private bath and walk-in closet.

plan# HPK2800086

First Floor: 1,493 sq. ft.
Second Floor: 676 sq. ft.
Total: 2,169 sq. ft.
Bedrooms: 3
Bathrooms: 2½
Width: 70' - 0"
Depth: 55' - 8"
Foundation: Crawlspace

ORDER ONLINE @ EPLANS.COM

FIRST FLOOR

SECOND FLOOR

plan# HPK2800087

Square Footage: 1,989
Bonus Space: 291 sq. ft.
Bedrooms: 3
Bathrooms: 2
Width: 80' - 6"
Depth: 50' - 0"
Foundation: Crawlspace

ORDER ONLINE @ EPLANS.COM

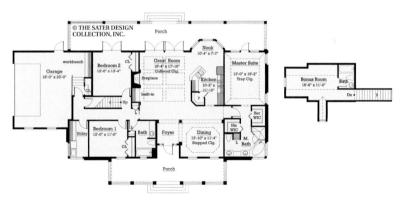

©The Sater Design Collection, Inc.

plan# HPK2800088

Square Footage: 1,989
Bonus Space: 274 sq. ft.
Bedrooms: 3
Bathrooms: 2
Width: 81' - 0"
Depth: 50' - 0"
Foundation: Crawlspace

ORDER ONLINE @ EPLANS.COM

©The Sater Design Collection, Inc.

plan# HPK2800089

Square Footage: 2,329
Bedrooms: 3
Bathrooms: 2½
Width: 72' - 0"
Depth: 73' - 10"
Foundation: Crawlspace

ORDER ONLINE @ EPLANS.COM

©The Sater Design Collection, Inc.

plan# HPK2800090

Square Footage: 2,487
Bedrooms: 3
Bathrooms: 2
Width: 70' - 0"
Depth: 72' - 0"
Foundation: Slab

ORDER ONLINE @ EPLANS.COM

Helpful Hint!

Reproducible sets include a license to build the home once.

© The Sater Design Collection, Inc.

plan # HPK2800091

First Floor: 1,819 sq. ft.
Second Floor: 638 sq. ft.
Total: 2,457 sq. ft.
Bonus Space: 385 sq. ft.
Bedrooms: 3
Bathrooms: 2½
Width: 47' - 4"
Depth: 82' - 8"
Foundation: Crawlspace, Unfinished Basement

ORDER ONLINE @ EPLANS.COM

Graceful dormers top a welcoming covered porch that is enhanced by Victorian details on this fine three-bedroom home. Inside, the foyer leads past the formal dining room back to the spacious two-story great room. Here, a fireplace, built-ins, and outdoor access make any gathering special. The nearby kitchen features a work island, a pantry, a serving bar, and an adjacent bayed breakfast area. Located on the first floor for privacy, the master suite is designed to pamper. Upstairs, two family bedrooms share a hall bath. Note the bonus space above the two-car garage.

FIRST FLOOR

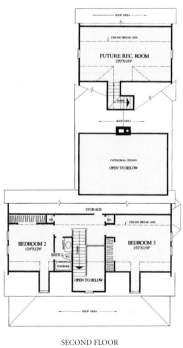

SECOND FLOOR

©2003 William E Poole Designs, Inc.

Delicate gingerbread details embellish the inviting porches of this gracious Queen Anne home. A formal yet open floor plan makes entertaining a thrill; at the front of the home the living room flows right into the dining room for special occasions; while beyond the staircase, an airy arrangement of skylit family room, vaulted breakfast nook, and spacious kitchen can accomodate more casual family gatherings and everyday activities. The master suite hides in a secluded corner of the main level. Upstairs, two family bedrooms share a bath and a loft area for reading and studying.

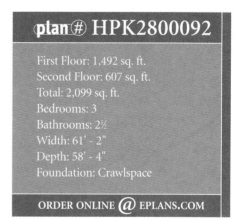

plan # HPK2800092

First Floor: 1,492 sq. ft.
Second Floor: 607 sq. ft.
Total: 2,099 sq. ft.
Bedrooms: 3
Bathrooms: 2½
Width: 61' - 2"
Depth: 58' - 4"
Foundation: Crawlspace

ORDER ONLINE @ EPLANS.COM

FIRST FLOOR

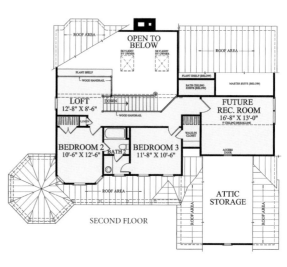

SECOND FLOOR

plan # HPK2800093

First Floor: 1,214 sq. ft.
Second Floor: 1,229 sq. ft.
Total: 2,443 sq. ft.
Bedrooms: 4
Bathrooms: 2½
Width: 52'- 4"
Depth: 55'- 10"
Foundation: Crawlspace, Unfinished
Walkout Basement

ORDER ONLINE @ EPLANS.COM

Inside this charming cottage you'll find a spacious, open floor plan that is perfect for entertaining. Fireplaces in the family room and keeping room combine to warm the adjoining kitchen and breakfast area. The practical design is ideal for family interaction. French doors lead to a screened porch, an option for outdoor dining or socializing. Upstairs, the master suite features tray ceilings and French door entry into the master bath. Once inside, the master bath boasts a dual sink vanity, a garden tub, a compartmented shower and toilet, and an enormous walk-in closet, with the option for a second. Three additional family bedrooms, sharing a full bath, complete the second floor.

FIRST FLOOR

SECOND FLOOR

copyright © 2004 frank betz associates, inc.

Fish-scale shingles, a weathervane, cupola, and covered wraparound veranda complete with Victorian touches make this farmhouse a truly memorable sight. The great room includes a fireplace for those chilly evenings and accesses the porch, perfect for warmer nights. The kitchen/breakfast area—island included—accesses the garage. All three bedrooms reside on the second floor. The master bedroom suite has a vaulted ceiling and access to a private deck. A unique sitting area is located on the landing between Bedrooms 2 and 3.

plan# HPK2800095

First Floor: 1,024 sq. ft.
Second Floor: 904 sq. ft.
Total: 1,928 sq. ft.
Bedrooms: 3
Bathrooms: 2½
Width: 65' - 0"
Depth: 35' - 5"
Foundation: Crawlspace, Unfinished Basement

ORDER ONLINE @ EPLANS.COM

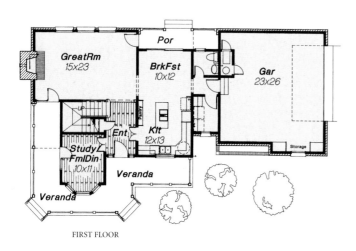

FIRST FLOOR

SECOND FLOOR

plan# HPK2800096

First Floor: 1,082 sq. ft.
Second Floor: 838 sq. ft.
Total: 1,920 sq. ft.
Bedrooms: 3
Bathrooms: 2½
Width: 66' - 10"
Depth: 29' - 5"
Foundation: Crawlspace, Slab,
Unfinished Basement

ORDER ONLINE @ EPLANS.COM

Farmhouse fresh with a touch of Victorian style best describes this charming home. A covered front porch wraps around the dining room's bay window and leads the way to the entrance. To the right of the entry is a living room that features a wet bar and a warming fireplace. At the rear of the plan, an L-shaped kitchen is equipped with an island cooktop, making meal preparation a breeze. Casual meals can be enjoyed in a dining area, which merges with the kitchen and accesses the rear patio. A powder room and utility room complete the first floor. Sleeping quarters contained on the second floor include a relaxing master suite with a large walk-in closet, two family bedrooms, and a connecting bath.

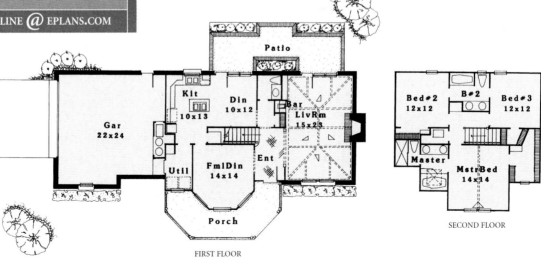

FIRST FLOOR

SECOND FLOOR

HELPFUL HINT! | Call one of our home plan experts about our customization services. Make your plan perfect.

Country and Victorian elements give this plan a down-home feel. A charming porch wraps around the front of this farmhouse, whose entry opens to a formal dining room. The island kitchen and sun-filled breakfast area are located nearby. The family room is warmed by a fireplace flanked by windows. Located for privacy, the first-floor master bedroom features its own covered patio and a private bath designed for relaxation. The second floor contains three family bedrooms—each with walk-in closets—a full bath, and a future bonus room.

plan# HPK2800097

First Floor: 1,572 sq. ft.
Second Floor: 700 sq. ft.
Total: 2,272 sq. ft.
Bonus Space: 212 sq. ft.
Bedrooms: 4
Bathrooms: 2½
Width: 70' - 0"
Depth: 38' - 5"
Foundation: Slab, Unfinished Basement

ORDER ONLINE @ EPLANS.COM

FIRST FLOOR

SECOND FLOOR

plan# HPK2800098

Square Footage: 2,293
Bonus Space: 536 sq. ft.
Bedrooms: 4
Bathrooms: 3
Width: 88' - 0"
Depth: 51' - 9"
Foundation: Slab, Unfinished Basement

ORDER ONLINE @ EPLANS.COM

Special gatherings and events will take place in the heart of this splendid home. The great room, defined by columns, includes a hearth and views to the covered patio. The east wing is occupied by the sleeping quarters, with a master bedroom which features an exclusive master bath. Two family bedrooms both have walk-in closets and share a compartmented bath with twin vanities. The three-car garage opens to the hall where the utility room, the kitchen, and an additional bedroom/study can be accessed. A future bonus room is also available upstairs.

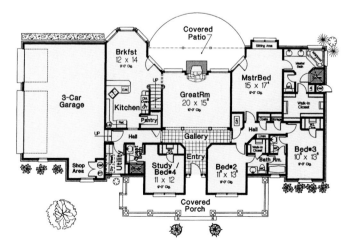

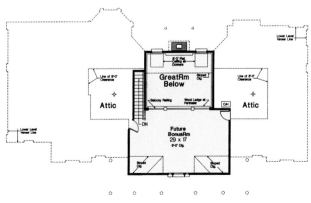

This country home displays Folk Victorian flair, with the large front gable decorated by fish-scale shingles. A wraparound porch and Palladian window topped by a keystone also highlight the home's exterior. Inside, notable features include a two-story living room warmed by a fireplace and a spacious master suite with a private sitting area, walk-in closet, and master bath. The kitchen serves the breakfast nook and formal dining room with ease. Upstairs, two additional bedrooms share a hall bath. An optional game room offers extra space.

plan# HPK2800094

First Floor: 1,848 sq. ft.
Second Floor: 537 sq. ft.
Total: 2,385 sq. ft.
Bonus Space: 361 sq. ft.
Bedrooms: 3
Bathrooms: 2½
Width: 61' - 3"
Depth: 59' - 6"
Foundation: Crawlspace, Slab, Unfinished Basement

ORDER ONLINE @ EPLANS.COM

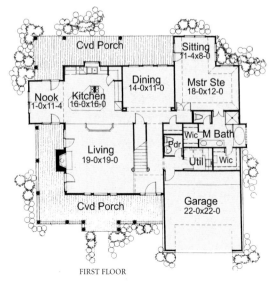

FIRST FLOOR

SECOND FLOOR

MORE THAN
2,500 SQUARE FEET

Victorian homes of the later 19th Century took a turn for the affluent and propagated the styles we know today as Second Empire, Richardsonian Romanesque, and Queen Anne. Wealthy homeowners elaborated on Victorian precedents, adding mansard roofs, shingles, and robust chimneys. As a result, the architecture of the Victorian home grew even more romantic and lavish—and more difficult to place into discrete subcategories. Today, competing trends of the period, such as the Craftsman style, also influence the Victorian identity.

Inside the home, the floor plan left the gates of conservative design and began to regard more irregular shapes. Of course, square footages increased; such as in the homes within this section, bedrooms and entertaining areas grew in size and importance. Homeowners wanted to treat themselves and their guests to all the delights of a grand Victorian home.

Take advantage of all the outdoor opportunities that come with your new home by choosing a complementing landscape plan. Select a full-flowering garden with water features and picnic areas, or a modest, no-fuss bit of greenery for your vacation home. To learn how to find a landscape plan that matches your new home, call our customer service center.

If you've dreamed about living in a classic Victorian home with all the modern amenities, this is the house for you. Complete with a front tower, a captain's deck, and a wraparound porch this is an impressive plan. The two-story entry hallway leads into a comfortable living area that includes a great room with a fireplace flanked by windows. To the right, a kitchen that will delight any chef, if only for the ample counter space, is located between a dining room and breakfast area with a wall of windows. The upstairs master suite is regal in its grandeur. Most striking is the oversize tub located in the tower and surrounded by three windows. The master bedroom enjoys a bay window, also with three windows. Two other bedrooms share a bath.

plan# HPK2800099

First Floor: 1,266 sq. ft.
Second Floor: 1,482 sq. ft.
Total: 2,748 sq. ft.
Bedrooms: 3
Bathrooms: 2½
Width: 42' - 6"
Depth: 50' - 6"
Foundation: Crawlspace

ORDER ONLINE @ EPLANS.COM

FIRST FLOOR

LAUN.

GREAT ROOM
16-0 X 20-6

BREAKFAST

UP

ENTRY HALL

DINING ROOM
13-0 X 14-0

SECOND FLOOR

BEDROOM
12-0 X 16-0

BEDROOM
11-6 X 13-0

DOWN

MASTER
BEDROOM
13-0 X 17-0

plan # HPK2800100

First Floor: 2,506 sq. ft.
Second Floor: 2,315 sq. ft.
Total: 4,821 sq. ft.
Bonus Space: 278 sq. ft.
Bedrooms: 5
Bathrooms: 4
Width: 60' - 0"
Depth: 97' - 0"
Foundation: Crawlspace

ORDER ONLINE @ EPLANS.COM

The lacy veranda that embraces the exterior of this Queen Anne home offers outdoor living space under its shady recesses. Inside, the great room features a fireplace, built-in shelves, and a wet bar. The kitchen boasts a walk-in pantry, an island countertop, a breakfast nook with a bayed window, and access to the keeping room and the rear covered porch. The second floor contains three family bedrooms and the master suite. The elegant master suite features a sitting area located within a turret, a spacious walk-in closet, an enormous bath with a step-up tub and dual vanities, and access to its own private exercise room. This home is designed with a two-car garage.

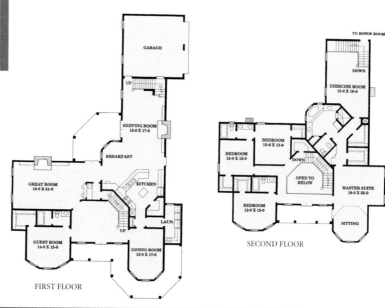

FIRST FLOOR

SECOND FLOOR

HELPFUL HINT! A materials list outlines your home's building materials, simplifying your cost-to-build estimate.

A Victorian beauty! With an impressive front-corner tower, bay windows, and a circular chimney with a decorative top, the exterior radiates grandeur. Formal entertaining will be done in the front dining and great rooms. Nearby is a guest bedroom with a bath for overnight guests. To the rear is the family area: a large keeping room, bayed breakfast alcove, and a kitchen surrounded by counter space. Upstairs, the deluxe master suite is what you've always dreamed about. The sleeping area is set in a huge bay with four windows; the oversize garden tub is also set in a bay lighted by three windows. There is also a shower, dual sinks, and a closeted toilet. Three other bedrooms are located on this level; one has a private bath, the other two share a bath. They all have walk-in closets.

plan⊕# HPK2800101

First Floor: 1,578 sq. ft.
Second Floor: 1,418 sq. ft.
Total: 2,996 sq. ft.
Bedrooms: 5
Bathrooms: 4
Width: 42' - 0"
Depth: 56' - 0"
Foundation: Crawlspace

ORDER ONLINE @ EPLANS.COM

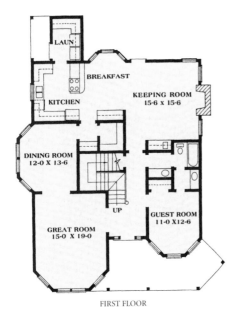

FIRST FLOOR

SECOND FLOOR

plan # HPK2800102

First Floor: 1,812 sq. ft.
Second Floor: 779 sq. ft.
Total: 2,591 sq. ft.
Bedrooms: 4
Bathrooms: 3½
Width: 47' - 0"
Depth: 78' - 0"
Foundation: Crawlspace

ORDER ONLINE @ EPLANS.COM

This stylish country home is especially well-designed for entertaining. Guests enter a covered front porch through two handsome pillars into a foyer that opens into a layout where one room appears to flow into another. To the left, the living room opens into the dining room, and straight ahead, a spacious great room opens to the kitchen with an island snack bar and sun-washed breakfast nook. A roomy butler's pantry is conveniently located between the kitchen and formal dining area. Two suites—one downstairs, the other upstairs—each enjoy private baths. The downstairs master suite enjoys both a shower and tub and dual His and Hers sinks. The upstairs sleeping area offers plenty of comfort for sleepover guests. A laundry and half-bath on the main floor complete this plan.

FIRST FLOOR

SECOND FLOOR

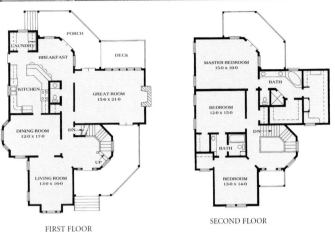

FIRST FLOOR

SECOND FLOOR

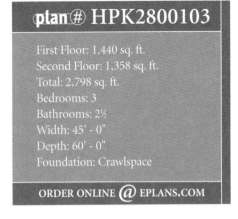

plan# HPK2800103

First Floor: 1,440 sq. ft.
Second Floor: 1,358 sq. ft.
Total: 2,798 sq. ft.
Bedrooms: 3
Bathrooms: 2½
Width: 45' - 0"
Depth: 60' - 0"
Foundation: Crawlspace

ORDER ONLINE @ EPLANS.COM

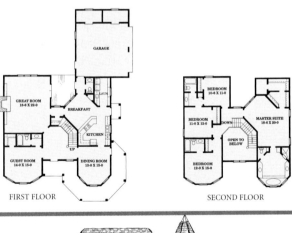

FIRST FLOOR

SECOND FLOOR

plan# HPK2800104

First Floor: 1,614 sq. ft.
Second Floor: 1,447 sq. ft.
Total: 3,061 sq. ft.
Bedrooms: 5
Bathrooms: 4½
Width: 52' - 0"
Depth: 76' - 0"
Foundation: Crawlspace

ORDER ONLINE @ EPLANS.COM

Welcome home to an elegant design taken straight from the history books. A wraparound porch with a gazebo corner plus a tall central tower give the facade distinct Victorian appeal. The angled entrance opens to a staircase, with the dining room on the right and formal living room and hallway on the left. Down the hallway, find the great room with central fireplace and a kitchen with a snack bar. Three windows warm the breakfast nook, and the pantry offers valued food storage. Upstairs, the master suite dominates the right side of the home, with a broad bedroom, a comfortable sitting area, a long bathroom, and an accomodating walk-in closet. Two additional bedrooms each has its own walk-in closet and vanity and shares a corner bathroom.

FIRST FLOOR

SECOND FLOOR

A glorious Queen Anne-style exterior hides all the requirements of a modern lifestyle as well as some charming features of earlier times. An octagonal tower is the focal point of the home, housing a unique entry hall. The hall opens to the living room, where a gas fireplace nestles into a corner between banks of windows. A built-in hutch highlights the dining room, and bookshelves slide open to reveal a secret stair leading to the second floor laundry! Other surprises include a discreet four-car garage and a mudroom to collect the clutter of today's busy families. The large kitchen, with a second sink in its central island, easily accommodates multiple cooks. Informal meals can be served on the terrace or in the sunny nook, which opens to the family room. This voluminous space is enhanced by a 14-foot ceiling and walls of windows. Upstairs, the master suite enjoys a corner fireplace, tower sitting room, and private deck.

plan# HPK2800106

First Floor: 2,027 sq. ft.
Second Floor: 1,430 sq. ft.
Total: 3,457 sq. ft.
Bedrooms: 3
Bathrooms: 3
Width: 98' - 7"
Depth: 72' - 6"
Foundation: Crawlspace

ORDER ONLINE @ EPLANS.COM

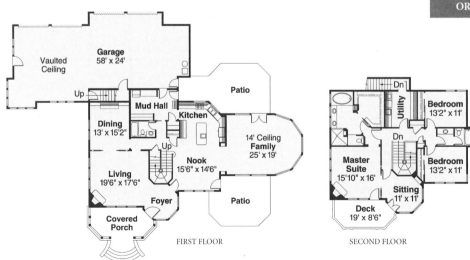

FIRST FLOOR

SECOND FLOOR

HELPFUL HINT! Eplans.com offers an Electrical Details set with residential electrical system information and diagrams.

plan# HPK2800107

First Floor: 3,162 sq. ft.
Second Floor: 1,595 sq. ft.
Total: 4,757 sq. ft.
Bonus Space: 2,651 sq. ft.
Bedrooms: 3
Bathrooms: 3½
Width: 110' - 2"
Depth: 68' - 11"
Foundation: Finished Basement, Slab

ORDER ONLINE @ EPLANS.COM

Victorian and Craftsman styles blend and create an inviting and detailed home. A two-story turret houses a second-floor reading room and first-floor master sitting bay. The dining and living areas are open and convenient to the rear porch and gourmet kitchen. An interior fountain divides the breakfast area and the spacious family room. The first-floor master suite features a corner fireplace and private bath. Family quarters, including two bedrooms and a large library, can be found on the second floor. Storage for holiday items and large keepsakes is also provided. On the lower level, a magnificent auto gallery, complete with a special car elevator, is perfect for the auto enthusiast in the family.

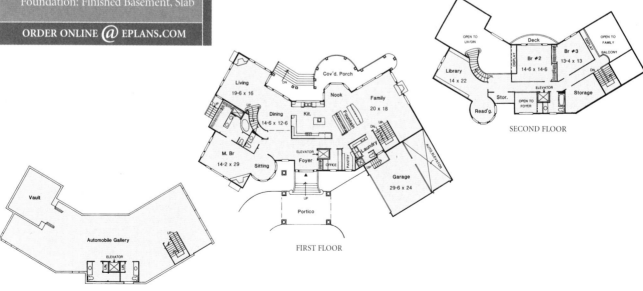

© Larry E. Belk Designs

With equally appealing front and side entrances, a charming Victorian facade invites entry to this stunning home. The foyer showcases the characteristic winding staircase and opens to the large great room with masonry fireplace. An enormous kitchen features a cooktop island and a breakfast bar large enough to seat four. A lovely bay window distinguishes the nearby dining room. The master suite with masonry fireplace is located on the first floor. The amenity-filled master bath features double vanities, a whirlpool tub, a separate shower, and a gigantic walk-in closet with an additional cedar closet. The second floor contains two bedrooms—one with access to the outdoor balcony on the side of the home. The third floor is completely expandable.

plan# HPK2800108

First Floor: 2,194 sq. ft.
Second Floor: 870 sq. ft.
Total: 3,064 sq. ft.
Bonus Space: 251 sq. ft.
Bedrooms: 3
Bathrooms: 2½
Width: 50' - 11"
Depth: 91' - 2"
Foundation: Crawlspace

ORDER ONLINE @ EPLANS.COM

FIRST FLOOR

SECOND FLOOR

ORDER BLUEPRINTS ANYTIME AT EPLANS.COM OR 1-800-521-6797

© Larry E. Belk Designs

plan# HPK2800109

First Floor: 1,329 sq. ft.
Second Floor: 1,917 sq. ft.
Third Floor: 189 sq. ft.
Total: 3,435 sq. ft.
Bedrooms: 3
Bathrooms: 2½
Width: 40' - 4"
Depth: 62' - 0"
Foundation: Slab

ORDER ONLINE @ EPLANS.COM

While speaking clearly of the past, the inside of this Victorian home coincides with the open, flowing interiors of today. Have meals in the elegant dining room with its tray ceiling, or move through the double French doors between the formal living room and informal family room to sense the comfort of this charming home. The kitchen boasts a large pantry and a corner sink with a window. The lovely master suite resides upstairs. The raised sitting area off the master bedroom provides the owner with a mini retreat for reading and relaxing. The second floor also includes two large bedrooms and a library/music room.

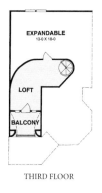

THIRD FLOOR

SECOND FLOOR

FIRST FLOOR

© Larry E. Belk Designs

Unusual rooflines characterize this four-bedroom family design. The front porch, with a gazebo-style sitting area, adds a country touch. Interior space begins with an entrance leading directly through the two-story foyer to a living room with a vaulted ceiling and a fireplace with flanking built-ins. The snack-bar kitchen easily serves the dining and breakfast rooms. The combined breakfast and keeping room is warmed by a fireplace and accesses the rear porch through double doors. The master bedroom is also warmed by a fireplace and boasts a luxurious master bath with His and Hers walk-in closets. A study/office is located nearby. On the opposite side of the home, a bay-windowed guest bedroom offers private access to a hall bath. Upstairs, Bedrooms 3 and 4 have their own baths and walk-in closets. A balcony overlooking the breakfast/keeping room leads to a loft area that accesses an expandable game room.

plan# HPK2800110

First Floor: 3,211 sq. ft.
Second Floor: 1,246 sq. ft.
Total: 4,457 sq. ft.
Bonus Space: 731 sq. ft.
Bedrooms: 4
Bathrooms: 4½
Width: 87' - 2"
Depth: 90' - 6"
Foundation: Crawlspace

ORDER ONLINE @ EPLANS.COM

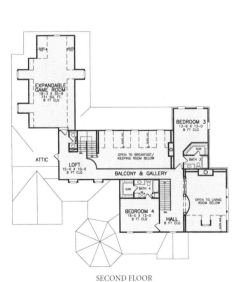

SECOND FLOOR

FIRST FLOOR

plan# HPK2800111

First Floor: 1,632 sq. ft.
Second Floor: 1,188 sq. ft.
Total: 2,820 sq. ft.
Bedrooms: 3
Bathrooms: 2 ½
Width: 61' - 3"
Depth: 68' - 6"
Foundation: Slab

ORDER ONLINE @ EPLANS.COM

This Victorian farmhouse is distinct because of its ornate detailing, including the decorative pinnacle, covered porch, and front-facing chimney. The living room is graced with a fireplace, wet bar, and tray ceiling. The family room also includes some appreciated amenities: an entertainment center, built-in bookshelves, and access to the covered patio. Upstairs, both the master suite and Bedroom 2 easily access a deck, and all bedrooms sport spacious walk-in closets. Ample attic space is also available for storage.

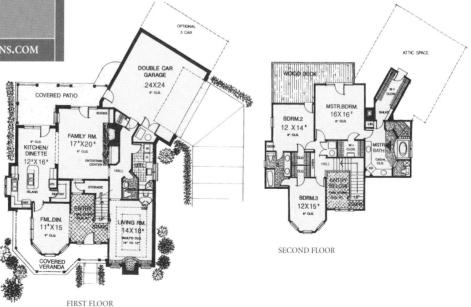

FIRST FLOOR

SECOND FLOOR

HELPFUL HINT! | Found a plan you *almost* love? A customization estimate for $50 is money well spent.

A wraparound porch makes this unique Victorian farmhouse stand out with style and grace, as does the lovely detailing of this plan. This design is versatile enough to accommodate either a small or large family. The entry is flanked on the left side by a large kitchen/breakfast area with an island, and on the right side by a parlor/music room. The family room is enhanced with a bar ledge, fireplace, and built-in entertainment center. The master suite has access to a covered deck. The upstairs level is shared by three bedrooms, two full baths, and a bonus room. A 448-square-foot apartment is located over the garage.

plan# HPK2800112

First Floor: 2,023 sq. ft.
Second Floor: 749 sq. ft.
Total: 2,772 sq. ft.
Bonus Space: 242 sq. ft.
Bedrooms: 5
Bathrooms: 4½
Width: 77' - 2"
Depth: 57' - 11"
Foundation: Slab, Unfinished Basement

ORDER ONLINE @ EPLANS.COM

SECOND FLOOR

FIRST FLOOR

plan# HPK2800113

Square Footage: 2,787
Bonus Space: 636 sq. ft.
Bedrooms: 4
Bathrooms: 2½
Width: 101' - 0"
Depth: 58' - 8"
Foundation: Crawlspace, Slab

ORDER ONLINE @ EPLANS.COM

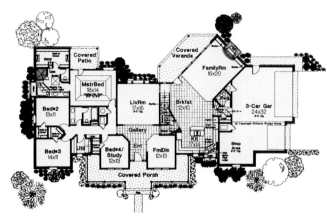

plan# HPK2800114

Square Footage: 3,439
Bonus Space: 514 sq. ft.
Bedrooms: 4
Bathrooms: 3½
Width: 100' - 0"
Depth: 67' - 11"
Foundation: Crawlspace, Slab,
Unfinished Basement

ORDER ONLINE @ EPLANS.COM

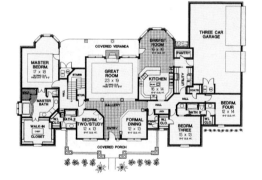

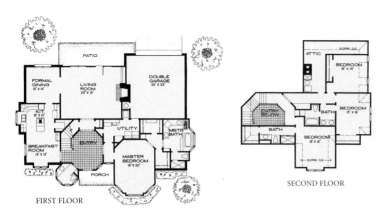

FIRST FLOOR

SECOND FLOOR

plan# HPK2800115

First Floor: 2,046 sq. ft.
Second Floor: 1,111 sq. ft.
Total: 3,157 sq. ft.
Bedrooms: 4
Bathrooms: 3½
Width: 65' - 8"
Depth: 51' - 11"
Foundation: Slab, Unfinished Basement

ORDER ONLINE @ EPLANS.COM

FIRST FLOOR

SECOND FLOOR

plan# HPK2800116

First Floor: 1,770 sq. ft.
Second Floor: 736 sq. ft.
Total: 2,506 sq. ft.
Bedrooms: 4
Bathrooms: 2½
Width: 46' - 10"
Depth: 74' - 2"
Foundation: Slab

ORDER ONLINE @ EPLANS.COM

plan# HPK2800118

First Floor: 1,120 sq. ft.
Second Floor: 1,411 sq. ft.
Total: 2,531 sq. ft.
Bedrooms: 4
Bathrooms: 2½
Width: 57' - 4"
Depth: 33' - 0"

ORDER ONLINE @ EPLANS.COM

Victorian detailing lends this four-bedroom home eye-catching charm, with fish-scale shingles, pinnacles and gingerbread decoration on the gables. To the left of the entry, a formal dining room provides space for a hutch. Across the entry, the living room's double doors open to the family room and its warming fireplace. Sharing the open space with the living room are a bay-windowed breakfast nook and kitchen. This kitchen will please any cook, with an island workstation, a pantry and a window over the sink. Tucked upstairs, away from everyday noises, four bedrooms all include walk-in closets. The master bedroom is complete with a tray ceiling, whirlpool bath, shower, dual vanity sinks and a compartmented toilet.

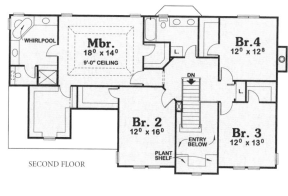

SECOND FLOOR

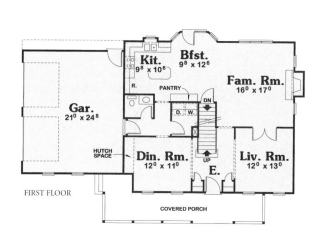

FIRST FLOOR

FIRST FLOOR

SECOND FLOOR

plan# HPK2800117

First Floor: 1,729 sq. ft.
Second Floor: 847 sq. ft.
Total: 2,576 sq. ft.
Bedrooms: 4
Bathrooms: 3½
Width: 84' - 8"
Depth: 51' - 9"

ORDER ONLINE @ EPLANS.COM

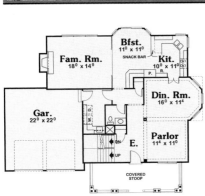

FIRST FLOOR

SECOND FLOOR

plan# HPK2800119

First Floor: 1,240 sq. ft.
Second Floor: 1,283 sq. ft.
Total: 2,523 sq. ft.
Bedrooms: 3
Bathrooms: 2½
Width: 56' - 0"
Depth: 38' - 8"

ORDER ONLINE @ EPLANS.COM

Helpful Hint!

Want to Mirror Reverse a design? It's an easy change to make for only $55.

plan# HPK2800120

First Floor: 2,142 sq. ft.
Second Floor: 673 sq. ft.
Total: 2,815 sq. ft.
Bonus Space: 455 sq. ft.
Bedrooms: 4
Bathrooms: 3
Width: 57' - 4"
Depth: 55' - 10"
Foundation: Crawlspace, Slab

ORDER ONLINE @ EPLANS.COM

Family unity and tradition come together. A generous great room provides the perfect setting for family movie night. Preparing meals will be a breeze, and serving them will be just as simple with the adjoining breakfast and dining rooms—both with bay windows. The master suite is nestled in the rear of this home on the main level. The upper floor offers beautiful balcony views of the great room and the foyer, as well as two more bedrooms and a media room option.

FIRST FLOOR

SECOND FLOOR

FIRST FLOOR   SECOND FLOOR

plan# HPK2800121

First Floor: 1,440 sq. ft.
Second Floor: 1,515 sq. ft.
Total: 2,955 sq. ft.
Bedrooms: 3
Bathrooms: 2 ½
Width: 39' - 2"
Depth: 69' - 5"
Foundation: Crawlspace

ORDER ONLINE @ EPLANS.COM

FIRST FLOOR   SECOND FLOOR

plan# HPK2800122

First Floor: 1,379 sq. ft.
Second Floor: 1,304 sq. ft.
Total: 2,683 sq. ft.
Bedrooms: 4
Bathrooms: 2 ½
Width: 54' - 8"
Depth: 61' - 4"
Foundation: Slab

ORDER ONLINE @ EPLANS.COM

plan# HPK2800123

First Floor: 2,041 sq. ft.
Second Floor: 1,098 sq. ft.
Total: 3,139 sq. ft.
Bonus Space: 385 sq. ft.
Bedrooms: 4
Bathrooms: 3½
Width: 76' - 6"
Depth: 62' - 2"
Foundation: Slab

ORDER ONLINE @ EPLANS.COM

FIRST FLOOR

SECOND FLOOR

plan# HPK2800124

First Floor: 1,474 sq. ft.
Second Floor: 1,554 sq. ft.
Total: 3,028 sq. ft.
Bedrooms: 4
Bathrooms: 3½
Width: 76' - 8"
Depth: 52' - 8"
Foundation: Slab

ORDER ONLINE @ EPLANS.COM

FIRST FLOOR

SECOND FLOOR

An abundance of muntin windows and a shingle facade are the defining characteristics of this design. Inside, the dining room is graced with French doors to the covered front porch. A home office flanks the foyer on the right. The master bedroom boasts a full bath, His and Hers walk-in closets, and French-door access to the rear covered porch. The grand room flows into the nook and kitchen. The second level holds two family bedrooms that share a lavish walk-through bath. A large future bonus room and a loft complete this level. The third floor houses a spacious attic/storage room.

plan# HPK2800125

First Floor: 2,376 sq. ft.
Second Floor: 1,078 sq. ft.
Total: 3,454 sq. ft.
Bonus Space: 549 sq. ft.
Bedrooms: 3
Bathrooms: 2½
Width: 80' - 6"
Depth: 85' - 6"
Foundation: Slab

ORDER ONLINE @ EPLANS.COM

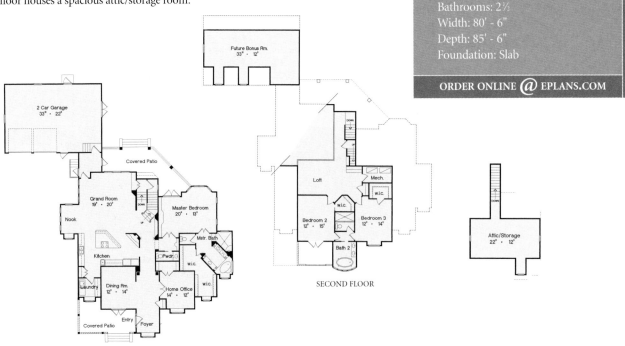

FIRST FLOOR

SECOND FLOOR

plan# HPK2800126

First Floor: 1,694 sq. ft.
Second Floor: 925 sq. ft.
Total: 2,619 sq. ft.
Bedrooms: 4
Bathrooms: 3½
Width: 57' - 0"
Depth: 50' - 9"
Foundation: Crawlspace, Slab,
Unfinished Basement

ORDER ONLINE @ EPLANS.COM

This home features all of the classic details that have made the Victorian style such a timeless design. The oversized front porch will welcome visitors day after day with its wood-turned posts, gingerbread trim, and cozy gazebo area. The entry views the formal dining area and parlor. An inviting family room features a warm fireplace, built-in media center, and bay window that views the rear yard. The breakfast nook is easily accessed by the family room and also features a rear-viewing bay window. The private master suite boasts a bay window and a luxurious bath. The master bath features a large marble tub, glass shower, and two walk-in closets. On the upper level, find three additional bedrooms, two full baths, a reading nook, and ample storage space.

FIRST FLOOR

SECOND FLOOR

HELPFUL HINT! The Right-Reading Reverse option flips the design but lets the on-plan text read correctly.

This two-story home offers you four-bedrooms and 2,782 square feet of living space. The unique character of this home is captivating. The great room features a see-through fireplace and surrounding built-in cabinets, along with two-story windows that overlook the backyard. From here, pass through a doorway into the kitchen to find a convenient walk-in pantry and island snack bar. A door from the kitchen leads through a mudroom and laundry room to the three-stall garage. Take a right from the foyer and discover a den and a master suite, each with double doors. The master bedroom will astonish with its remarkable master bath and walk-in closet. Taking the stairs to the second floor, find the other three bedrooms along with a bridge that overlooks the great room and foyer. All three bedrooms benefit from large closets and two bathrooms.

plan # HPK2800127

First Floor: 1,912 sq. ft.
Second Floor: 870 sq. ft.
Total: 2,782 sq. ft.
Bedrooms: 4
Bathrooms: 3 ½
Width: 69' - 4"
Depth: 62' - 0"
Foundation: Unfinished Basement

ORDER ONLINE @ EPLANS.COM

FIRST FLOOR

SECOND FLOOR

plan# HPK2800128

First Floor: 1,865 sq. ft.
Second Floor: 1,155 sq. ft.
Total: 3,020 sq. ft.
Bedrooms: 4
Bathrooms: 3½
Width: 63' - 4"
Depth: 64' - 8"
Foundation: Unfinished Basement

ORDER ONLINE @ EPLANS.COM

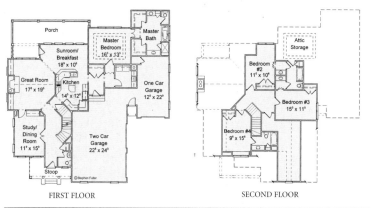

FIRST FLOOR   SECOND FLOOR

plan# HPK2800129

First Floor: 2,277 sq. ft.
Second Floor: 1,044 sq. ft.
Total: 3,321 sq. ft.
Bonus Space: 211 sq. ft.
Bedrooms: 5
Bathrooms: 4
Width: 76' - 0"
Depth: 51' - 0"
Foundation: Unfinished Basement

ORDER ONLINE @ EPLANS.COM

FIRST FLOOR   SECOND FLOOR

The charming exterior of this one-of-a-kind home features exquisite architectural details set off by a romantic massing and a warm blend of materials. The first floor provides a secluded guest room that offers private access to a full bath. Stunning formal rooms frame the foyer—a perfect arrangement for entertaining. To the rear of the plan, a spacious great room offers a fireplace and splendid views of the rear property. Upstairs, magnificent amenities enrich the master suite, including a fireplace, garden tub, knee-space vanity, and walk-in closet designed for two. A balcony hall leads to two family bedrooms, a laundry, and a guest suite.

plan # HPK2800130

First Floor: 1,709 sq. ft.
Second Floor: 1,958 sq. ft.
Total: 3,667 sq. ft.
Bedrooms: 5
Bathrooms: 4
Width: 59' - 4"
Depth: 63' - 6"
Foundation: Unfinished Walkout Basement

ORDER ONLINE @ EPLANS.COM

FIRST FLOOR

SECOND FLOOR

plan# HPK2800131

First Floor: 2,864 sq. ft.
Second Floor: 2,329 sq. ft.
Total: 5,193 sq. ft.
Bedrooms: 4
Bathrooms: 4½ + ½
Width: 64' - 6"
Depth: 87' - 6"
Foundation: Unfinished Walkout
Basement

ORDER ONLINE @ EPLANS.COM

At nearly 5,200 square feet, this French Country beauty is replete with luxurious amenities inside that match the elegance outside. Formal living spaces are made contemporary with upgraded ceiling treatments and abundant space. The expansive great room is ideal for social gatherings with convenient access to the rear back porch. To the left, the first-floor master bedroom enjoys privacy and seclusion. Upstairs, the three family bedrooms each boast a full bath. Friends and family alike will indulge in the ever popular media room. The adjacent half-bath is a thoughtful accomodation for guests. A discreet, side-loading three-car garage adds curb appeal.

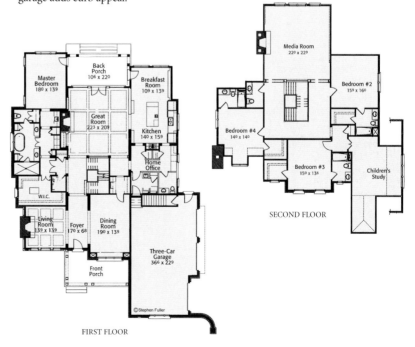

Screened Porch

Great Room
23⁹x14⁶

Two Car Garage
21⁹x24³

Breakfast
15⁵x8³

Kitchen
15⁵x9³

Dining Room
14⁵x14⁰

Guest/ Study
15⁵x12⁰

Porch

FIRST FLOOR

Master Bedroom
23⁹x16⁰

W.I.C.

Master Bath

Unfinished Bonus
15⁵x14⁰

W.I.C.

Bedroom No. 3
15⁵x11⁰

Bedroom No. 2
15⁵x11³

SECOND FLOOR

Porch

Two Car Garage
23⁹x23³

Kitchen

Breakfast
12⁵x13³

13⁵x15³

Dining Room
15⁵x12³

Great Room
15⁵x22³

Living Room
15⁵x12³

Foyer

Porch

FIRST FLOOR

Bedroom No. 2
12⁵x11³

Bedroom No. 3
13⁵x11³

Master Bedroom
15⁵x21⁹

Open to Below

Bedroom No. 4
12⁵x13⁰

SECOND FLOOR

Helpful Hint!

Want to move the garage? Reverse the plan or modify it!

plan # HPK2800131

First Floor: 2,864 sq. ft.
Second Floor: 2,329 sq. ft.
Total: 5,193 sq. ft.
Bedrooms: 4
Bathrooms: 4½ + ½
Width: 64' - 6"
Depth: 87' - 6"
Foundation: Unfinished Walkout Basement

ORDER ONLINE @ EPLANS.COM

At nearly 5,200 square feet, this French Country beauty is replete with luxurious amenities inside that match the elegance outside. Formal living spaces are made contemporary with upgraded ceiling treatments and abundant space. The expansive great room is ideal for social gatherings with convenient access to the rear back porch. To the left, the first-floor master bedroom enjoys privacy and seclusion. Upstairs, the three family bedrooms each boast a full bath. Friends and family alike will indulge in the ever popular media room. The adjacent half-bath is a thoughtful accomodation for guests. A discreet, side-loading three-car garage adds curb appeal.

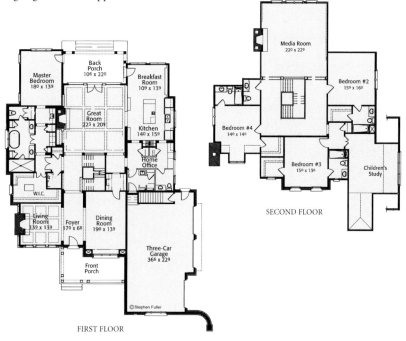

SECOND FLOOR

FIRST FLOOR

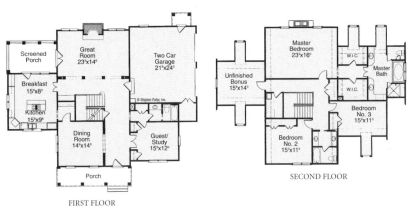

FIRST FLOOR

SECOND FLOOR

plan # HPK2800132

First Floor: 1,634 sq. ft.
Second Floor: 1,598 sq. ft.
Total: 3,232 sq. ft.
Bonus Space: 273 sq. ft.
Bedrooms: 4
Bathrooms: 3
Width: 62' - 0"
Depth: 54' - 9"
Foundation: Finished Walkout Basement

ORDER ONLINE @ EPLANS.COM

FIRST FLOOR

SECOND FLOOR

plan # HPK2800133

First Floor: 1,613 sq. ft.
Second Floor: 1,546 sq. ft.
Total: 3,159 sq. ft.
Bedrooms: 4
Bathrooms: 3 ½
Width: 69' - 0"
Depth: 57' - 0"
Foundation: Finished Walkout Basement

ORDER ONLINE @ EPLANS.COM

Helpful Hint!

Want to move the garage? Reverse the plan or modify it!

plan# HPK2800134

First Floor: 2,628 sq. ft.
Second Floor: 1,775 sq. ft.
Total: 4,403 sq. ft.
Bedrooms: 5
Bathrooms: 3 ½
Width: 79' - 6"
Depth: 65' - 1"
Foundation: Unfinished Walkout Basement

ORDER ONLINE @ EPLANS.COM

With five bedrooms and a wonderful stone-and-siding exterior, this country home will satisfy every need. Two sets of French doors provide access to the dining room and foyer. The great room enjoys a warming fireplace and deck access. The kitchen, breakfast bay, and keeping room feature an open floor plan. A charming sitting area in a bay window sets off the master bedroom. The master bath features a large walk-in closet, two-sink vanity, separate tub and shower, and compartmented toilet. Four bedrooms, an office, and two full baths complete the upper level.

REAR EXTERIOR

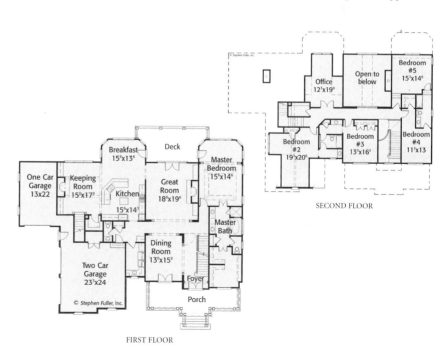

FIRST FLOOR

SECOND FLOOR

FIRST FLOOR

SECOND FLOOR

plan# HPK2800135

First Floor: 1,734 sq. ft.
Second Floor: 1,091 sq. ft.
Total: 2,825 sq. ft.
Bonus Space: 488 sq. ft.
Bedrooms: 4
Bathrooms: 3½
Width: 57' - 6"
Depth: 80' - 11"
Foundation: Crawlspace, Unfinished Basement

ORDER ONLINE @ EPLANS.COM

FIRST FLOOR

SECOND FLOOR

plan# HPK2800136

First Floor: 2,442 sq. ft.
Second Floor: 1,286 sq. ft.
Total: 3,728 sq. ft.
Bonus Space: 681 sq. ft.
Bedrooms: 4
Bathrooms: 3½ + ½
Width: 84' - 8"
Depth: 60' - 0"
Foundation: Crawlspace

ORDER ONLINE @ EPLANS.COM

© William E. Poole Designs, Inc.

plan# HPK2800137

First Floor: 1,480 sq. ft.
Second Floor: 1,651 sq. ft.
Total: 3,131 sq. ft.
Bedrooms: 4
Bathrooms: 3½
Width: 67' - 5"
Depth: 61' - 5"
Foundation: Crawlspace

ORDER ONLINE @ EPLANS.COM

This design incorporates Victorian touches with the masterful use of a turret and a gazebo. With a wealth of windows, this home never lacks natural light. Inside, divergent room shapes offer interesting appeal. The family room is centrally located with a fireplace and a built-in entertainment center on the left wall. The island kitchen features a built-in desk, abundant counter space, and a butler's pantry. A separate utility room houses the washer/dryer, fold-down ironing board, and sink. The second floor houses the sleeping quarters, including the lavish master suite, complete with a private sitting area and fireplace, and three additional family bedrooms sharing two full baths.

SECOND FLOOR

FIRST FLOOR

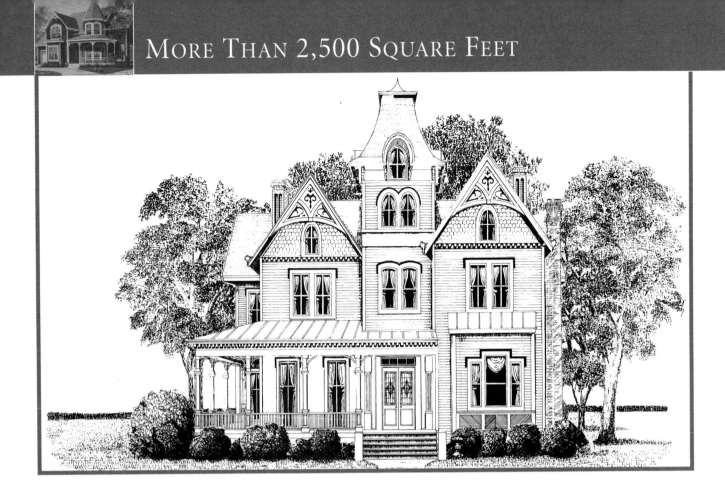

A turn-of-the-century style meets turn-of-the-millenium convenience in a traditional Victorian design. The front porch wraps around one corner, providing entrances to both the foyer and the breakfast nook. Three separate fireplaces each warm the home's living room, dining room, and great room. An island kitchen has plenty of counter space for small or large meal preparation, while cabinet-covered walls keep any preparatory messes well hidden from guests. The second floor houses the sleeping quarters: two family bedrooms with a shared full bath, one bedroom with a private bath, and the master suite. The master bath is couple-ready, with a double vanity and twin walk-in closets.

plan# HPK2800138

First Floor: 1,582 sq. ft.
Second Floor: 1,854 sq. ft.
Total: 3,436 sq. ft.
Bedrooms: 4
Bathrooms: 3 ½
Width: 48' - 0"
Depth: 68' - 0"
Foundation: Crawlspace

ORDER ONLINE @ EPLANS.COM

FIRST FLOOR

SECOND FLOOR

plan# HPK2800139

First Floor: 1,726 sq. ft.
Second Floor: 1,613 sq. ft.
Total: 3,339 sq. ft.
Bedrooms: 4
Bathrooms: 3½
Width: 63' - 0"
Depth: 70' - 0"
Foundation: Crawlspace

ORDER ONLINE @ EPLANS.COM

FIRST FLOOR

SECOND FLOOR

plan# HPK2800140

First Floor: 1,408 sq. ft.
Second Floor: 1,194 sq. ft.
Total: 2,602 sq. ft.
Bedrooms: 4
Bathrooms: 2½
Width: 38' - 0"
Depth: 50' - 0"
Foundation: Crawlspace

ORDER ONLINE @ EPLANS.COM

Helpful Hint!

Want to hide the garage entrance? A minor plan modification may allow a side-load garage.

FIRST FLOOR

SECOND FLOOR

FIRST FLOOR

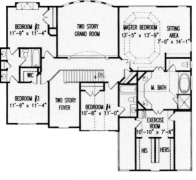

SECOND FLOOR

plan# HPK2800141

First Floor: 1,578 sq. ft.
Second Floor: 1,543 sq. ft.
Total: 3,121 sq. ft.
Bedrooms: 5
Bathrooms: 4
Width: 53' - 0"
Depth: 40' - 0"
Foundation: Unfinished Walkout Basement

ORDER ONLINE @ EPLANS.COM

FIRST FLOOR

SECOND FLOOR

plan# HPK2800142

First Floor: 1,649 sq. ft.
Second Floor: 1,604 sq. ft.
Total: 3,253 sq. ft.
Bedrooms: 4
Bathrooms: 3 ½
Width: 54' - 0"
Depth: 45' - 8"
Foundation: Slab, Unfinished Walkout Basement

ORDER ONLINE @ EPLANS.COM

plan# HPK2800143

First Floor: 1,417 sq. ft.
Second Floor: 1,169 sq. ft.
Total: 2,586 sq. ft.
Bonus Space: 119 sq. ft.
Bedrooms: 4
Bathrooms: 2½
Width: 52' - 0"
Depth: 43' - 6"
Foundation: Slab, Unfinished
Basement, Unfinished Walkout
Basement

ORDER ONLINE @ EPLANS.COM

A wraparound covered porch welcomes you to this efficient two-story home. Inside, the formal rooms open directly off the foyer, and the two-story grand room is toward the rear. A private study is available for home office space. The U-shaped kitchen features a work island and an adjacent breakfast area. Upstairs, three family bedrooms share a full bath and an overlook to the grand room. The deluxe master suite offers a large private bath, huge walk-in closet, and an optional sitting area.

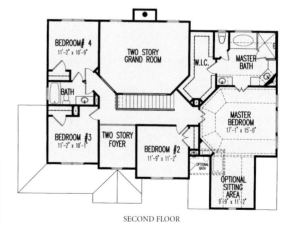

SECOND FLOOR

FIRST FLOOR

A variety of facade textures add interest and curb appeal to this two-story home. The covered front porch welcomes friends and family to the elegant front door and on into the two-story foyer. Here a formal dining room and a formal living room wait to either side. Past the U-shaped staircase, the spacious kitchen provides a pantry, cooktop island with a serving bar, and plenty of counter and cabinet space. The adjacent breakfast area opens into the two-story family room, separated by a decorative column. A study/bedroom completes this floor. Upstairs, Bedrooms 3 and 4 share a full bath, while Bedroom 2 offers privacy with its own bath. The master suite is complete with a sitting area, fireplace, built-ins, and a lavish bath.

plan⊕ HPK2800144

First Floor: 1,577 sq. ft.
Second Floor: 1,689 sq. ft.
Total: 3,266 sq. ft.
Bedrooms: 5
Bathrooms: 4½
Width: 59' - 4"
Depth: 49' - 0"
Foundation: Crawlspace, Unfinished Walkout Basement

ORDER ONLINE @ EPLANS.COM

FIRST FLOOR

SECOND FLOOR

plan# HPK2800145

First Floor: 2,224 sq. ft.
Second Floor: 1,030 sq. ft.
Total: 3,254 sq. ft.
Bedrooms: 4
Bathrooms: 3
Width: 65' - 4"
Depth: 53' - 8"
Foundation: Crawlspace, Unfinished
Walkout Basement

ORDER ONLINE @ EPLANS.COM

FIRST FLOOR   SECOND FLOOR

plan# HPK2800146

First Floor: 2,182 sq. ft.
Second Floor: 980 sq. ft.
Total: 3,162 sq. ft.
Bedrooms: 4
Bathrooms: 3½
Width: 70' - 4"
Depth: 65' - 0"
Foundation: Crawlspace, Slab,
Unfinished Walkout Basement

ORDER ONLINE @ EPLANS.COM

FIRST FLOOR   SECOND FLOOR

© 1991 Donald A. Gardner Architects, Inc.

Imagine entertaining in this fantastic living room. It's octagonal shape offers a perfect place to gather and mingle. Windows line five of the eight walls, and additional light shines in from the windows in the clerestory above. A fireplace highlights a sixth wall, beyond which lies the formal dining room. This room is easily served by the spacious and open kitchen, which combines with the family room and the breakfast nook to create a cozy, casual gathering space. The bay-windowed master suite also resides on the first floor; a classically Victorian covered porch surrounds all. Upstairs are three family bedrooms and two baths.

plan# HPK2800147

First Floor: 1,790 sq. ft.
Second Floor: 792 sq. ft.
Total: 2,582 sq. ft.
Bedrooms: 4
Bathrooms: 3½
Width: 63' - 0"
Depth: 80' - 4"

ORDER ONLINE @ EPLANS.COM

FIRST FLOOR

SECOND FLOOR

HELPFUL HINT! Head to ebuild.com for a wide array of doors, windows, lighting, cabinets, and flooring.

© 1992 Donald A. Gardner Architects, Inc.

plan# HPK2800148

First Floor: 1,381 sq. ft.
Second Floor: 1,135 sq. ft.
Total: 2,516 sq. ft.
Bonus Space: 422 sq. ft.
Bedrooms: 4
Bathrooms: 2½
Width: 68' - 1"
Depth: 43' - 8"

ORDER ONLINE @ EPLANS.COM

A two-story country-style home may be exactly what you are looking for to entertain guests in southern style and accommodate a growing family. When visitors pass through the welcoming columns on the front porch into the foyer, they know this is a special place. To the right is the formal dining room, and straight ahead is the great room with a centered fireplace. The island kitchen easily serves the dining room and the sunlit breakfast nook. The second floor houses four bedrooms—including the master suite—and a bonus room.

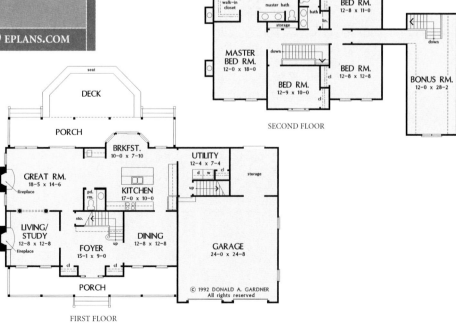

SECOND FLOOR

FIRST FLOOR

plan# HPK2800149

Square Footage: 2,934
Bedrooms: 4
Bathrooms: 3
Width: 85' - 4"
Depth: 57' - 8"

ORDER ONLINE @ EPLANS.COM

MAIN LEVEL

LOWER LEVEL

plan# HPK2800150

Main Level: 1,732 sq. ft.
Lower Level: 920 sq. ft.
Total: 2,652 sq. ft.
Bedrooms: 3
Bathrooms: 3
Width: 70' - 6"
Depth: 59' - 6"

ORDER ONLINE @ EPLANS.COM

plan# HPK2800151

First Floor: 1,848 sq. ft.
Second Floor: 799 sq. ft.
Total: 2,647 sq. ft.
Bonus Space: 457 sq. ft.
Bedrooms: 3
Bathrooms: 3½
Width: 81' - 0"
Depth: 49' - 8"

ORDER ONLINE @ EPLANS.COM

Circle-head transoms and decorative brackets soften strong angled gables, and bold columns define a welcoming country porch. Service entries from the garage, deck, and utility/mud room create convenience. Inside, a curved balcony separates the two-story foyer and great room, which is marked by columns at the entrance and warmed by a fireplace. A bay window extends the breakfast nook, which is adjacent to the island kitchen. The first-floor master suite is well appointed, and the master bath is complete with a dual-sink vanity, separate tub and shower, and nearby walk-in closets. Both second-floor bedrooms have their own private baths. This home is equipped with a bonus room, and outdoor living space is abundant.

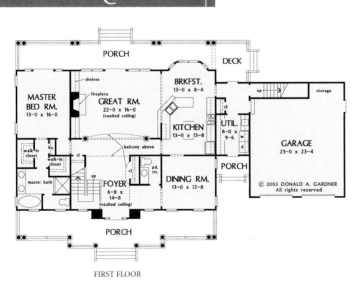

FIRST FLOOR

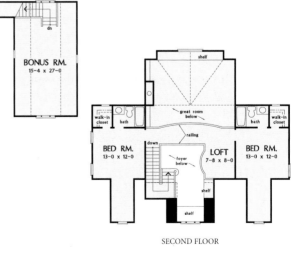

SECOND FLOOR

This beautiful farmhouse, with its prominent twin gables and bays, adds just the right amount of country style. The master suite is quietly tucked away downstairs with no rooms directly above. The family cook will love the spacious U-shaped kitchen and adjoining bayed breakfast nook. A bonus room awaits expansion on the second floor, where three large bedrooms share two full baths. Storage space abounds with walk-ins, half-shelves, and linen closets. A curved balcony borders a versatile loft/study, which overlooks the stunning two-story family room.

plan# HPK2800152

First Floor: 2,086 sq. ft.
Second Floor: 1,077 sq. ft.
Total: 3,163 sq. ft.
Bonus Space: 403 sq. ft.
Bedrooms: 4
Bathrooms: 3½
Width: 81' - 10"
Depth: 51' - 8"

ORDER ONLINE @ EPLANS.COM

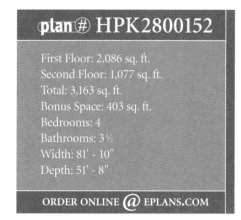

SECOND FLOOR

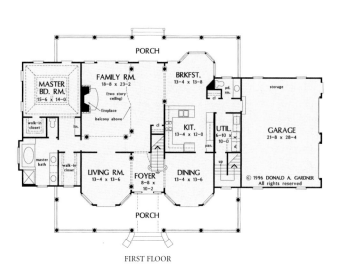

FIRST FLOOR

plan# HPK2800153

First Floor: 1,459 sq. ft.
Second Floor: 1,554 sq. ft.
Total: 3,013 sq. ft.
Bedrooms: 4
Bathrooms: 3½
Width: 60' - 0"
Depth: 48' - 0"
Foundation: Unfinished Basement

ORDER ONLINE @ EPLANS.COM

An elegant Victorian design with a columned front porch, this two-story home has lots of curb appeal. Inside you'll find two second-floor master suites with walk-in closets and pampering baths, plus two family bedrooms, a full hall bath, and a convenient laundry room. The main level is just as roomy with a large kitchen and eating bar, a walk-in pantry, and a breakfast room that opens onto a large deck. The formal dining and living rooms are wonderfully positioned to make entertaining a breeze. The family room features a warming fireplace and offers access to the front porch.

SECOND FLOOR

FIRST FLOOR

FIRST FLOOR

SECOND FLOOR

plan# HPK2800154

First Floor: 1,842 sq. ft.
Second Floor: 739 sq. ft.
Total: 2,581 sq. ft.
Bonus Space: 379 sq. ft.
Bedrooms: 3
Bathrooms: 4½
Width: 79' - 0"
Depth: 50' - 0"
Foundation: Crawlspace

ORDER ONLINE @ EPLANS.COM

©The Sater Design Collection, Inc.

FIRST FLOOR

SECOND FLOOR

plan# HPK2800155

First Floor: 1,834 sq. ft.
Second Floor: 732 sq. ft.
Total: 2,556 sq. ft.
Bedrooms: 3
Bathrooms: 4½
Width: 79' - 0"
Depth: 50' - 0"
Foundation: Crawlspace

ORDER ONLINE @ EPLANS.COM

©The Sater Design Collection, Inc.

©The Sater Design Collection, Inc.

plan # HPK2800156

First Floor: 1,373 sq. ft.
Second Floor: 1,581 sq. ft.
Total: 2,954 sq. ft.
Bedrooms: 4
Bathrooms: 2½
Width: 64' - 6"
Depth: 52' - 2"
Foundation: Crawlspace

ORDER ONLINE @ EPLANS.COM

Brick and siding, along with a multitude of other delightful details, combine to give this home plenty of curb appeal. The oval windows on the French entry doors are wonderfully complemented by the columned porch—which is perfect for relaxing on breezy summer evenings. The foyer leads straight to the stepped-ceiling leisure room, which features built-ins and a grand hearth. An L-shaped kitchen offers an island and connecting space to the brightly lit breakfast nook. The sleeping quarters are located on the second level. The master suite has a private master deck, a whirlpool tub, and His and Hers walk-in closets. Family bedrooms share a dual-vanity bath.

SECOND FLOOR

FIRST FLOOR

©The Sater Design Collection, Inc.

The symmetry of this home indicates Colonial roots. Double pediments sit above the porch entry. The octagonal-shaped great room is the heart of the home, separating the master quarters from the living zones. The open dining room enjoys a stepped ceiling and convenience to the island kitchen. Access to the rear porch is found just off the dining room. Two bedrooms with private baths, a loft and a den complete the second level of this home.

plan # HPK2800157

First Floor: 1,627 sq. ft.
Second Floor: 1,024 sq. ft.
Total: 2,651 sq. ft.
Bedrooms: 3
Bathrooms: 3½
Width: 78' - 6"
Depth: 80' - 6"
Foundation: Crawlspace

ORDER ONLINE @ EPLANS.COM

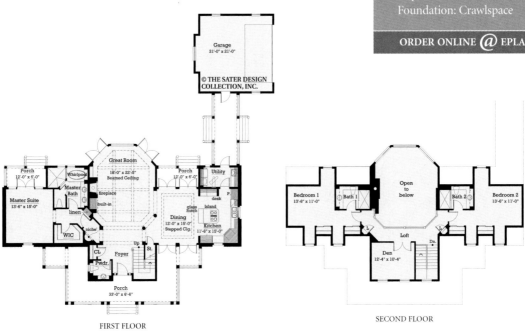

FIRST FLOOR

SECOND FLOOR

plan # HPK2800158

First Floor: 1,673 sq. ft.
Second Floor: 1,463 sq. ft.
Total: 3,136 sq. ft.
Bedrooms: 3
Bathrooms: 2½
Width: 60' - 10"
Depth: 62' - 0"
Foundation: Crawlspace

ORDER ONLINE @ EPLANS.COM

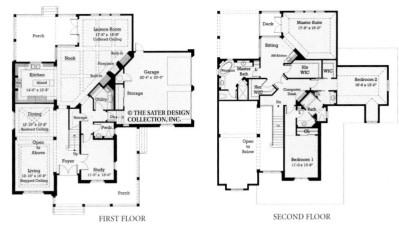

FIRST FLOOR   SECOND FLOOR

©The Sater Design Collection, Inc.

plan # HPK2800159

First Floor: 1,664 sq. ft.
Second Floor: 1,471 sq. ft.
Total: 3,135 sq. ft.
Bedrooms: 3
Bathrooms: 2½
Width: 60' - 10"
Depth: 62' - 0"
Foundation: Crawlspace

ORDER ONLINE @ EPLANS.COM

FIRST FLOOR   SECOND FLOOR

©The Sater Design Collection, Inc.

©The Sater Design Collection, Inc.

This quaint Colonial-style farmhouse will impress with its vast array of family-friendly amenities. Inside, the foyer is flanked by a study and formal dining room. Straight ahead, a fireplace flanked by built-ins warms the spacious great room. The gourmet island kitchen overlooks a casual nook. The master suite is a luxurious retreat featuring built-ins, a private whirlpool bath, and a huge walk-in closet. Upstairs, a loft overlooks the great room and nook below. Two family bedrooms share a Jack-and-Jill whirlpool bath. The bonus room is perfect for a guest suite or home office.

plan# HPK2800160

First Floor: 2,151 sq. ft.
Second Floor: 734 sq. ft.
Total: 2,885 sq. ft.
Bonus Space: 522 sq. ft.
Bedrooms: 3
Bathrooms: 2 ½
Width: 99' - 0"
Depth: 56' - 0"
Foundation: Crawlspace

ORDER ONLINE @ EPLANS.COM

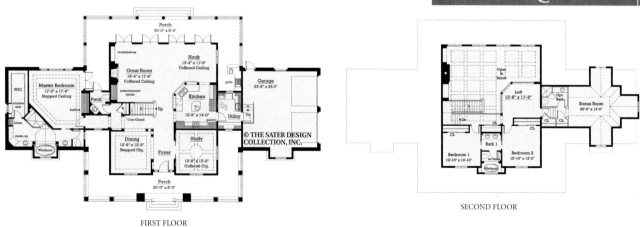

FIRST FLOOR

SECOND FLOOR

©The Sater Design Collection, Inc.

plan# HPK2800161

First Floor: 1,865 sq. ft.
Second Floor: 1,477 sq. ft.
Total: 3,342 sq. ft.
Bonus Space: 282 sq. ft.
Bedrooms: 4
Bathrooms: 2½
Width: 79' - 6"
Depth: 79' - 2"
Foundation: Crawlspace

ORDER ONLINE @ EPLANS.COM

Twin dormers, fish-scale shingles, and elegant columns create an eye-catching facade for this Victorian-style home. The formal living and dining rooms feature stately coffered ceilings, and a beamed ceiling accents the study. The living room also includes a fireplace. A leisure room, tailored for more casual times, includes several sets of French doors that open to the wrap-around rear porch, as well as built-in space for an entertainment center. Sleeping quarters fill the second floor—three family bedrooms and a luxurious master suite with a private sitting area, walk-in closet, and lavish bath. A "study hall" area offers a place to put the family computer.

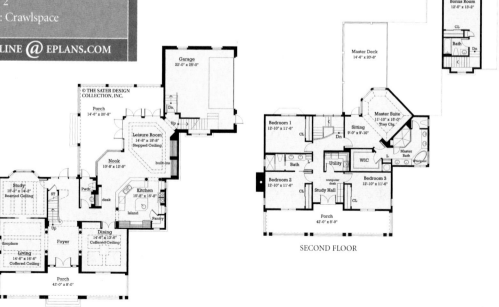

FIRST FLOOR

SECOND FLOOR

FIRST FLOOR

SECOND FLOOR

plan# HPK2800162

First Floor: 1,387 sq. ft.
Second Floor: 1,175 sq. ft.
Total: 2,562 sq. ft.
Bonus Space: 362 sq. ft.
Bedrooms: 3
Bathrooms: 2½
Width: 54' - 0"
Depth: 78' - 0"
Foundation: Crawlspace

ORDER ONLINE @ EPLANS.COM

FIRST FLOOR

SECOND FLOOR

plan# HPK2800163

First Floor: 1,387 sq. ft.
Second Floor: 1,175 sq. ft.
Total: 2,562 sq. ft.
Bonus Space: 362 sq. ft.
Bedrooms: 3
Bathrooms: 2½
Width: 54' - 6"
Depth: 78' - 6"
Foundation: Crawlspace

ORDER ONLINE @ EPLANS.COM

©The Sater Design Collection, Inc.

ptan# HPK2800164

First Floor: 2,215 sq. ft.
Second Floor: 708 sq. ft.
Total: 2,923 sq. ft.
Bonus Space: 420 sq. ft.
Bedrooms: 3
Bathrooms: 3
Width: 76' - 4"
Depth: 69' - 10"
Foundation: Crawlspace

ORDER ONLINE @ EPLANS.COM

Clean, simple lines define this Victorian-style home, which opens through double doors to a spacious grand room. Adornments here include a coffered ceiling and triple French doors to the covered porch at the back. Both the dining room and the master bedroom feature stepped ceilings. Two walk-in closets and a fine bath with a separate tub and shower further enhance the master suite. Both family bedrooms upstairs have walk-in closets and built-ins. A bonus room can become an additional bedroom later, with space for a full bath.

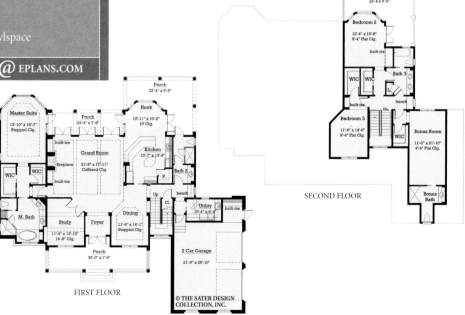

SECOND FLOOR

FIRST FLOOR

© THE SATER DESIGN COLLECTION, INC.

© The Sater Design Collection, Inc.

This English manor is sure to please, with its attractive facade and accommodating interior. The wraparound portico leads to the graceful foyer. Here, a formal dining room opens to the right and offers a refined ceiling treatment. The spacious great room provides a fireplace, built-ins, an entertainment center, and access to the rear veranda. The sumptuous kitchen provides a worktop island, a beamed ceiling, and a nearby bayed breakfast nook. The lavish, first-floor master suite is complete with a large, skylit walk-in closet, deluxe bath, and private access to the rear veranda. Upstairs, a computer loft separates the guest suite from the family bedrooms. Note the bonus room over the garage—perfect for another guest suite or maid's quarters.

plan # HPK2800165

First Floor: 2,219 sq. ft.
Second Floor: 1,088 sq. ft.
Total: 3,307 sq. ft.
Bonus Space: 446 sq. ft.
Bedrooms: 4
Bathrooms: 3 ½
Width: 91' - 0"
Depth: 52' - 8"
Foundation: Slab

ORDER ONLINE @ EPLANS.COM

FIRST FLOOR

SECOND FLOOR

©The Sater Design Collection, Inc.

plan# HPK2800166

First Floor: 2,096 sq. ft.
Second Floor: 892 sq. ft.
Total: 2,988 sq. ft.
Bedrooms: 3
Bathrooms: 3½
Width: 56' - 0"
Depth: 54' - 0"
Foundation: Unfinished Walkout
Basement

ORDER ONLINE @ EPLANS.COM

Siding and shingles give this home a Craftsman look while columns and gables suggest a more traditional style. The foyer opens to a short flight of stairs that leads to the great room, which features a lovely coffered ceiling, a fireplace, built-ins, and French doors to the rear veranda. To the left, the open, island kitchen enjoys a pass-through to the great room and easy service to the dining bay. The secluded master suite has two walk-in closets, a luxurious bath, and veranda access. Upstairs, two family bedrooms enjoy their own full baths and share a loft area.

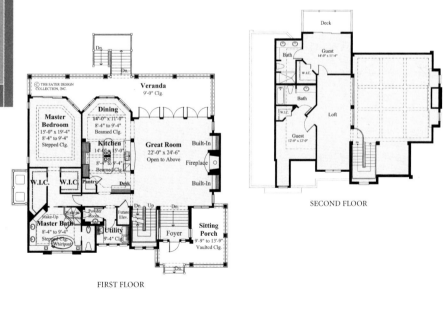

FIRST FLOOR

SECOND FLOOR

HELPFUL HINT! | Eplans.com offers a Plumbing Details set with general residential plumbing information and diagrams.

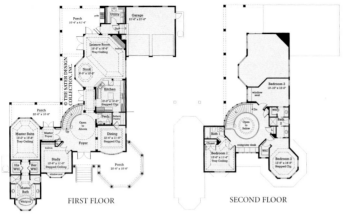

FIRST FLOOR   SECOND FLOOR

plan# HPK2800167

First Floor: 2,083 sq. ft.
Second Floor: 1,013 sq. ft.
Total: 3,096 sq. ft.
Bedrooms: 4
Bathrooms: 3½
Width: 74' - 0"
Depth: 88' - 0"
Foundation: Crawlspace

ORDER ONLINE @ EPLANS.COM

©The Sater Design Collection, Inc.

FIRST FLOOR   SECOND FLOOR

plan# HPK2800168

First Floor: 2,083 sq. ft.
Second Floor: 1,013 sq. ft.
Total: 3,096 sq. ft.
Bedrooms: 4
Bathrooms: 3½
Width: 59' - 6"
Depth: 88' - 0"
Foundation: Slab

ORDER ONLINE @ EPLANS.COM

©The Sater Design Collection, Inc.

plan# HPK2800169

First Floor: 2,083 sq. ft.
Second Floor: 1,013 sq. ft.
Total: 3,096 sq. ft.
Bedrooms: 4
Bathrooms: 3 ½
Width: 74' - 0"
Depth: 88' - 0"
Foundation: Crawlspace

ORDER ONLINE @ EPLANS.COM

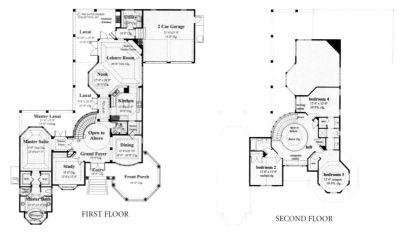

FIRST FLOOR   SECOND FLOOR

©The Sater Design Collection, Inc.

plan# HPK2800170

First Floor: 2,083 sq. ft.
Second Floor: 1,013 sq. ft.
Total: 3,096 sq. ft.
Bedrooms: 4
Bathrooms: 3 ½
Width: 74' - 0"
Depth: 88' - 6"
Foundation: Crawlspace

ORDER ONLINE @ EPLANS.COM

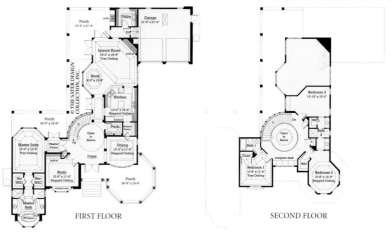

FIRST FLOOR   SECOND FLOOR

©The Sater Design Collection, Inc.

©The Sater Design Collection, Inc.

This luxurious vacation cabin is the perfect rustic paradise, whether set by a lake or a mountain scene. The wraparound entry porch is friendly and inviting. Double doors open into the foyer, that is flanked on either side by the study—with built-in cabinetry—and the formal dining room. The octagonal great room features a vaulted ceiling, a fireplace, and a built-in entertainment center. The gourmet island kitchen is brightened by a bayed window and a pass-through to the lanai. A set of private double doors opens to the vaulted master lanai. Two family bedrooms with private baths are featured upstairs. A computer center, a morning kitchen, and a second-floor deck are located at the end of the hall.

plan# HPK2800171

First Floor: 1,855 sq. ft.
Second Floor: 901 sq. ft.
Total: 2,756 sq. ft.
Bedrooms: 3
Bathrooms: 3½
Width: 66' - 0"
Depth: 50' - 0"
Foundation: Unfinished Walkout Basement

ORDER ONLINE @ EPLANS.COM

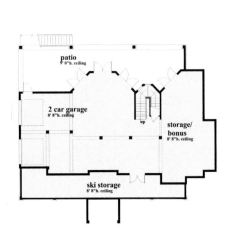

FIRST FLOOR

SECOND FLOOR

©The Sater Design Collection, Inc.

Tall windows wrap this noble exterior with dazzling details and allow plenty of natural light inside. A wraparound porch sets a casual but elegant pace for the home, with space for rockers and swings. Well-defined formal rooms are placed just off the foyer. A host of French doors opens the great room to an entertainment porch and inspiring views. Even formal meals take on the ease and comfort of a mountain region in the stunning open dining room. Nearby, a gourmet kitchen packed with amenities serves any occasion.

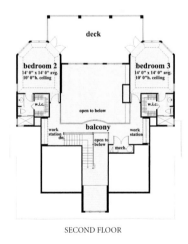

SECOND FLOOR

FIRST FLOOR

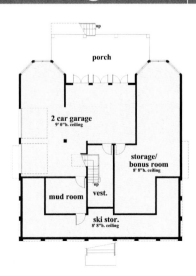

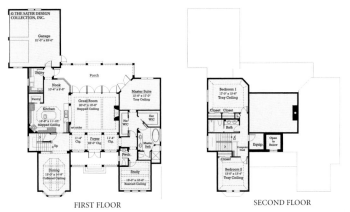

FIRST FLOOR   SECOND FLOOR

plan# HPK2800173

First Floor: 2,073 sq. ft.
Second Floor: 682 sq. ft.
Total: 2,755 sq. ft.
Bedrooms: 3
Bathrooms: 2½
Width: 64' - 0"
Depth: 76' - 2"
Foundation: Crawlspace

ORDER ONLINE @ EPLANS.COM

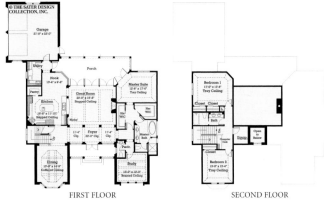

©The Sater Design Collection, Inc.

FIRST FLOOR   SECOND FLOOR

plan# HPK2800174

First Floor: 2,073 sq. ft.
Second Floor: 682 sq. ft.
Total: 2,755 sq. ft.
Bedrooms: 3
Bathrooms: 2½
Width: 64' - 6"
Depth: 76' - 8"
Foundation: Crawlspace

ORDER ONLINE @ EPLANS.COM

Helpful Hint!

We're the only plans seller with trained consultants available 24/7 to answer your questions.

©The Sater Design Collection, Inc.

© The Sater Design Collection, Inc.

plan # HPK2800175

Square Footage: 3,942
Bedrooms: 3
Bathrooms: 4
Width: 83' - 10"
Depth: 106' - 0"
Foundation: Slab

ORDER ONLINE @ EPLANS.COM

Welcome home to a country manor with Renaissance flair. Full-length, squint-style windows and brick accents bring Old World charm to a modern plan. Designed for flexibility, the open foyer, living room, and dining room have infinite decor options. Down a gallery (with art niches), two bedroom suites enjoy private baths. The bon-vivant island kitchen is introduced with a wet bar and pool bath. In the leisure room, family and friends will revel in expansive views of the rear property. An outdoor kitchen on the lanai invites alfresco dining. Separated for ultimate privacy, the master suite is an exercise in luxurious living. Past the morning kitchen and into the grand bedroom, an octagonal sitting area is bathed in light. The bath is gracefully set in the turret, with a whirlpool tub and views of the master garden.

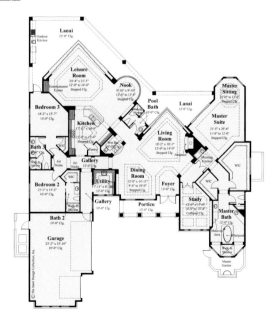

©The Sater Design Collection, Inc.

A comely exterior gives way to an open floor plan stocked with exceptional amenities. Upgraded ceiling treatments are found throughout, adding elegance. A fireplace in the leisure room is accentuated by built-in bookcases. Double French doors open to a rear porch, extending the living space outdoors. The island kitchen opens to the adjoining breakfast nook. Upstairs houses the sleeping quarters, including the luxurious master suite complete with private deck access, a make-up station, a whirlpool tub, and His and Hers amenities. Two secondary bedrooms share a Jack-and-Jill bath. Equipped with a full bath and a walk-in closet, the bonus room over the garage could serve as a guest suite or a future media room.

plan# HPK2800176

First Floor: 1,642 sq. ft.
Second Floor: 1,205 sq. ft.
Total: 2,847 sq. ft.
Bonus Space: 300 sq. ft.
Bedrooms: 3
Bathrooms: 2½
Width: 53' - 2"
Depth: 72' - 0"
Foundation: Crawlspace

ORDER ONLINE @ EPLANS.COM

FIRST FLOOR

SECOND FLOOR

©The Sater Design Collection, Inc.

plan # HPK2800177

First Floor: 1,642 sq. ft.
Second Floor: 1,205 sq. ft.
Total: 2,847 sq. ft.
Bonus Space: 340 sq. ft.
Bedrooms: 3
Bathrooms: 2½
Width: 53' - 7"
Depth: 72' - 6"
Foundation: Crawlspace

ORDER ONLINE @ EPLANS.COM

This impressive two-story farmhouse is a family delight. A wraparound front porch welcomes you inside to a foyer flanked on either side by a formal dining room and parlor. The leisure room is enhanced by a fireplace flanked by built-ins and a wall of double doors opening to the rear porch. The island kitchen overlooks the bayed nook. The second floor features a pampering master bedroom with a private second-floor deck, His and Hers walk-in closets, and a whirlpool master bath. Two additional bedrooms share a Jack-and-Jill bath. The bonus room above the garage is perfect for a guest suite or home office.

FIRST FLOOR

SECOND FLOOR

Rich with Victorian details—scalloped shingles, a wraparound veranda, and turrets—this beautiful facade conceals a modern floor plan. Archways announce a distinctive tray-ceilinged living room and help define the dining room. An octagonal den across from the foyer provides a private spot for reading or studying. The U-shaped island kitchen holds an octagonal breakfast bay and a pass-through breakfast bar to the family room. Upstairs, three family bedrooms share a hall bath—one bedroom is within a turret. The master suite is complete with a sitting room with a bay window, along with a fancy bath set in another of the turrets.

plan# HPK2800178

First Floor: 1,362 sq. ft.
Second Floor: 1,270 sq. ft.
Total: 2,632 sq. ft.
Bedrooms: 4
Bathrooms: 2 ½
Width: 79' - 0"
Depth: 44' - 0"
Foundation: Crawlspace, Unfinished Basement

ORDER ONLINE @ EPLANS.COM

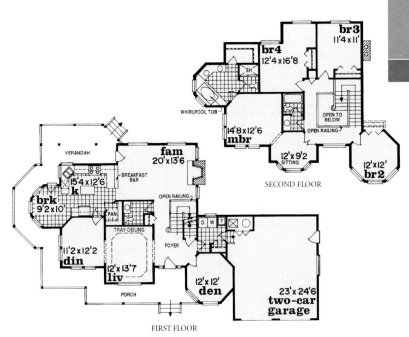

plan# HPK2800179

First Floor: 1,317 sq. ft.
Second Floor: 1,216 sq. ft.
Total: 2,533 sq. ft.
Bedrooms: 4
Bathrooms: 2 ½
Width: 65' - 0"
Depth: 44' - 0"
Foundation: Crawlspace, Unfinished Basement

ORDER ONLINE @ EPLANS.COM

Country elegance combined with a well-planned interior makes this a perfect family home. Nine-foot ceilings throughout the first level provide an enhanced feeling of spaciousness for living areas. The kitchen and breakfast nook serve as the hub of the first-floor plan. On the right, find the living room and formal dining room; on the left is the family room. Fireplaces warm both the living room and the family room. A private den is found just off the entry. The second floor holds three family bedrooms and a master suite with a private bath. A large workshop area sits in the garage.

FIRST FLOOR

SECOND FLOOR

HELPFUL HINT! Our hurricane relief program offers a free plan to anyone rebuilding after Katrina, Rita, and Wilma.

A touch of Victoriana enhances the facade of this home: a turret roof over a wrap-around porch with turned wood spindles. Special attractions on the first floor include a tray ceiling in the octagonal living room, fireplaces in the country kitchen and the living room, a coffered ceiling in the family room, and double-door access to the cozy den. The master suite, set in the upper level of the turret, boasts a coffered ceiling, walk-in closet, and whirlpool tub. Three family bedrooms and a full hall bath join the master suite on the second floor.

plan# HPK2800180

First Floor: 1,462 sq. ft.
Second Floor: 1,288 sq. ft.
Total: 2,750 sq. ft.
Bedrooms: 4
Bathrooms: 2½
Width: 70' - 8"
Depth: 54' - 0"
Foundation: Crawlspace, Unfinished Basement

ORDER ONLINE @ EPLANS.COM

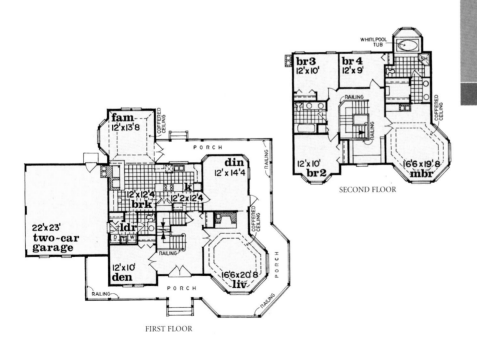

FIRST FLOOR

SECOND FLOOR

plan⊕ HPK2800181

First Floor: 1,324 sq. ft.
Second Floor: 1,192 sq. ft.
Total: 2,516 sq. ft.
Bedrooms: 4
Bathrooms: 2½
Width: 67' - 6"
Depth: 47' - 6"
Foundation: Crawlspace, Unfinished Basement

ORDER ONLINE @ EPLANS.COM

A turret, wood detailing, and a wraparound veranda signal desirable Victorian style for this home. The double-door entry opens to a foyer with a lovely curved staircase and leads into the living and dining rooms on the right and the den on the left. All three rooms have attractive tray ceilings. The living room boasts a fireplace, and the formal dining room features a buffet alcove. Sliding glass doors in the dining room open to the veranda. Four bedrooms occupy the second floor. A tray ceiling highlights the master suite, and the private bath and walk-in closet give it a luxurious feel. Bedroom 2 includes a cozy window seat.

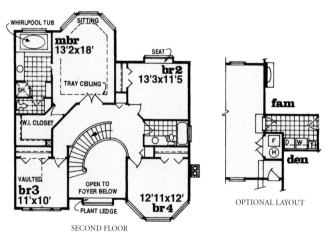

SECOND FLOOR

OPTIONAL LAYOUT

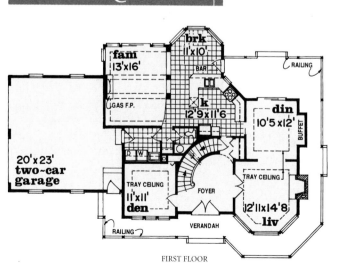

FIRST FLOOR

Entertaining is easy in this spacious four-bedroom home with an expansive U-shaped interior. From the foyer, an office with built-ins and a pass-through bar to the great room sits on the left; to the right is a formal dining room with a built-in hutch and a butler's pantry with wine closet. The kitchen includes counter space on three walls plus a center island with a sink and space for casual eating. The right wing consists of a four-bay garage, workshop area, and inset barbecue porch. In the opposite wing lies a guest room, pool bath, and master suite with His and Hers amenities. A convenient bonus is the pre-installed ironing board in the larger walk-in closet. Joining the home's two wings is the great room. Here, a built-in media center and access to the bar and the veranda make it an excellent room for entertaining or spending time with the family. Upstairs, two bedroom suites with built-in desks, walk-in closets, and private baths flank a flexible media/playroom area.

plan# HPK2800182

First Floor: 3,800 sq. ft.
Second Floor: 990 sq. ft.
Total: 4,790 sq. ft.
Bedrooms: 4
Bathrooms: 5½
Width: 116' - 0"
Depth: 88' - 0"
Foundation: Crawlspace

ORDER ONLINE @ EPLANS.COM

SECOND FLOOR

REAR EXTERIOR

FIRST FLOOR

plan# HPK2800183

First Floor: 2,572 sq. ft.
Second Floor: 1,578 sq. ft.
Total: 4,150 sq. ft.
Bonus Space: 315 sq. ft.
Bedrooms: 4
Bathrooms: 4½
Width: 78' - 2"
Depth: 68' - 0"
Foundation: Crawlspace

ORDER ONLINE @ EPLANS.COM

Craftsman detailing and a Victorian flair make this home a standout in any neighborhood. An impressive foyer opens to the left to the great room, with a coffered ceiling, warming fireplace, and a charming alcove set in a turret. The kitchen is designed for entertaining, with an island that doubles as a snack bar and plenty of room to move. An adjacent porch invites dining alfresco. The bayed study is peaceful and quiet. A nearby guest room includes a private bath. Upstairs, the master suite is awe-inspiring. A romantic fireplace sets the mood and natural light pours in. A sumptuous spa bath leaves homeowners pampered and relaxed. Two bedroom suites share a vaulted bonus room, perfect as a home gym.

SECOND FLOOR

FIRST FLOOR

Country Victoriana embellishes this beautiful home. Perfect for a corner lot, the home begs for porch swings and lemonade. Inside, extra-high ceilings expand the space as a thoughtful floor plan invites family and friends. The two-story great room enjoys a warming fireplace and wonderful rear views. The country kitchen has a preparation island and easily serves the sunny bayed nook and the formal dining room. To the far left, a bedroom serves as a perfect guest room; to the far right, a turret houses a private den. Upstairs, two bedrooms (one in a turret) share a full bath and ample bonus space. The master suite opens through French doors to reveal a grand bedroom and a sumptuous bath with a bumped-out spa tub.

plan # HPK2800184

First Floor: 1,464 sq. ft.
Second Floor: 1,054 sq. ft.
Total: 2,518 sq. ft.
Bonus Space: 332 sq. ft.
Bedrooms: 4
Bathrooms: 3
Width: 59' - 0"
Depth: 51' - 6"
Foundation: Crawlspace

ORDER ONLINE @ EPLANS.COM

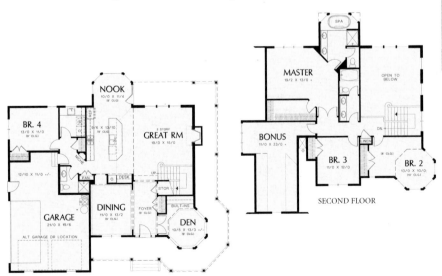

FIRST FLOOR

SECOND FLOOR

HELPFUL HINT! | Many of our plans come with optional landscape or deck plans.

164   ORDER BLUEPRINTS ANYTIME AT EPLANS.COM OR 1-800-521-6797

plan # HPK2800185

First Floor: 1,297 sq. ft.
Second Floor: 1,390 sq. ft.
Total: 2,687 sq. ft.
Bonus Space: 229 sq. ft.
Bedrooms: 3
Bathrooms: 2½
Width: 60' - 0"
Depth: 44' - 0"
Foundation: Unfinished Basement

ORDER ONLINE @ EPLANS.COM

A truly lavish master suite resides on the second floor of this complex two-story farmhouse. The recessed entry opens to the dining room and kitchen with the family room on the right. The massive wraparound porch can be accessed from the family room, living room, and the sunny breakfast bay. The island kitchen is conveniently placed between the dining room and the well-equipped utility room. On the second floor, the master suite enjoys a fireplace, a pampering bath, and access to the second-floor deck.

SECOND FLOOR

FIRST FLOOR

This striking example of Gothic Victorian design features curved porches, vergeboard trim, and finial-topped gables. To the left of the foyer is the formal dining room; to the right is a combination living room/family room with a bay window and a fireplace. The kitchen shares a snack bar with a small sitting or media room that opens to the covered back porch. Upstairs, three bedrooms—one with a walk-in closet—share a full bath that includes double vanities and a raised corner tub. Double doors in the hallway open to a balcony overlooking the front yard.

plan# HPK2800186

First Floor: 1,358 sq. ft.
Second Floor: 1,149 sq. ft.
Total: 2,507 sq. ft.
Bedrooms: 3
Bathrooms: 2
Width: 36' - 0"
Depth: 40' - 8"
Foundation: Unfinished Basement

ORDER ONLINE @ EPLANS.COM

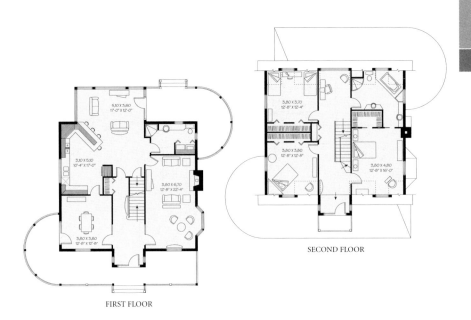

FIRST FLOOR

SECOND FLOOR

plan# HPK2800187

First Floor: 1,352 sq. ft.
Second Floor: 1,238 sq. ft.
Total: 2,590 sq. ft.
Bonus Space: 459 sq. ft.
Bedrooms: 3
Bathrooms: 2½
Width: 62' - 0"
Depth: 44' - 0"
Foundation: Unfinished Basement

ORDER ONLINE @ EPLANS.COM

A Victorian porch and turret embellish this otherwise modern country home with the style and charm of yesterday. A beautiful foyer with porch views greets family and friends, offering access to the living and dining rooms. Continue past a central powder room to the hearth-warmed family room. A well-equipped kitchen with a walk-in pantry is situated nearby and leads out to the rear porch. Upstairs, bedrooms are arranged with privacy in mind. The master suite revels in a resplendent bath and enormous walk-in closet. A two-car garage completes this special plan.

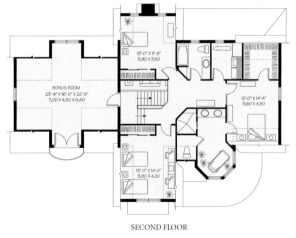

SECOND FLOOR

FIRST FLOOR

Uniquely shaped rooms and a cache of amenities highlight this three-story beauty. The large sunken family room features a fireplace, wet bar, and built-in seat. A liberal amount of work space is available in the kitchen, breakfast room with built-in desk, and laundry. A four-car garage easily holds the family fleet. The second floor contains two bedrooms and a full bath plus a master suite with His and Hers closets, multiple vanities, and a whirlpool bath. There's also a second-floor veranda. An exercise room on the third floor features its own sauna and bath, while the large guest room on this floor is complemented by a charming alcove and another full bath.

plan # HPK2800188

First Floor: 2,515 sq. ft.
Second Floor: 1,708 sq. ft.
Third Floor: 1,001 sq. ft.
Total: 5,224 sq. ft.
Bedrooms: 4
Bathrooms: 4½ + ½
Width: 90' - 6"
Depth: 60' - 0"
Foundation: Unfinished Basement

ORDER ONLINE @ EPLANS.COM

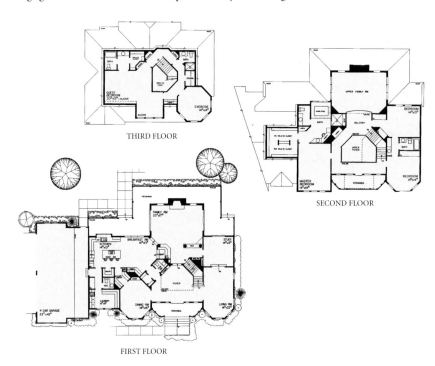

THIRD FLOOR

SECOND FLOOR

FIRST FLOOR

A magnificent covered porch wraps around this impressive Victorian estate home. The two-story foyer provides a direct view into the great room with a large central fireplace. To the left of the foyer is a bookshelf-lined library and to the right is an octagonal dining room. The island cooktop serves as a convenient work space in the kitchen, and a pass-through connects this room with the morning room. A luxurious master suite on the first floor opens to the rear covered porch. Four uniquely designed bedrooms, three full baths, and a lounge with a fireplace are located on the second floor.

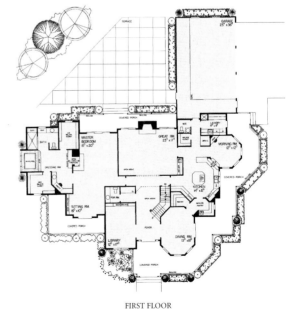

FIRST FLOOR

SECOND FLOOR

What could beat the charm of a turreted Victorian with covered porches to the front, side, and rear? This delicately detailed exterior houses an outstanding family-oriented floor plan. Projecting bays make their contribution to the exterior styling. In addition, they provide an extra measure of livability to the living, dining, and family rooms, plus two of the bedrooms. The efficient kitchen, with its island cooking station, functions well with the dining and family rooms. A study provides a quiet first-floor haven for the family's less-active pursuits. Upstairs, there are three big bedrooms and a fine master bath. The third floor provides a guest suite and huge bulk storage area (make it a cedar closet if you wish). This house has a basement for the development of further recreational and storage facilities. Note the two fireplaces, large laundry, and attached two-car garage.

plan# HPK2800190

First Floor: 1,618 sq. ft.
Second Floor: 1,315 sq. ft.
Third Floor: 477 sq. ft.
Total: 3,410 sq. ft.
Bedrooms: 4
Bathrooms: 3½
Width: 71' - 8"
Depth: 48' - 4"
Foundation: Unfinished Basement

ORDER ONLINE @ EPLANS.COM

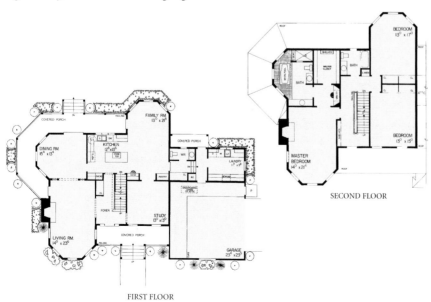

FIRST FLOOR

SECOND FLOOR

THIRD FLOOR

This home is a lovely example of classic Queen Anne architecture. Its floor plan offers a sunken gathering room with fireplace, a hearth-warmed study with turret sitting area, a formal dining room with fireplace, and a kitchen with attached breakfast room. A double staircase leads to the second floor, which includes a bedroom in each corner, with the grand master suite's two walk-in closets and island bath extending into the left wing. A sitting porch above the entry welcomes calming views of the front yard. On the third floor are a guest room with private bath and sitting room and a game room with attached library.

THIRD FLOOR

SECOND FLOOR

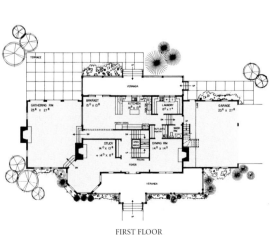

FIRST FLOOR

This beautiful Folk Victorian has all the properties of others in its class. Living areas include a formal Victorian parlor, a private study, and large gathering room. The formal dining room has its more casual counterpart in a bay-windowed breakfast room. Both are near the well-appointed kitchen. Five bedrooms serve family and guest needs handily; three are on the second floor and two more are on the third floor. The master suite includes a bath with whirlpool tub, separate shower, and two sinks. For outdoor entertaining there is a covered rear porch leading to a terrace. The two-car garage is arranged to the rear of the home and attaches to the main house at a service entrance near the laundry and mudroom.

plan# HPK2800192

First Floor: 1,683 sq. ft.
Second Floor: 1,388 sq. ft.
Third Floor: 808 sq. ft.
Total: 3,879 sq. ft.
Bedrooms: 5
Bathrooms: 3½
Width: 64' - 0"
Depth: 67' - 0"
Foundation: Unfinished Basement

ORDER ONLINE @ EPLANS.COM

THIRD FLOOR

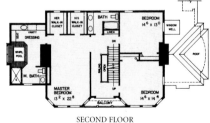

SECOND FLOOR

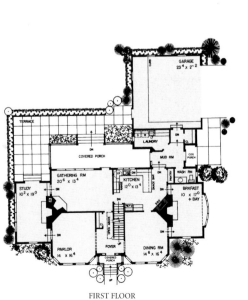

FIRST FLOOR

plan# HPK2800193

First Floor: 1,517 sq. ft.
Second Floor: 1,267 sq. ft.
Third Floor: 480 sq. ft.
Total: 3,264 sq. ft.
Bedrooms: 4
Bathrooms: 3½
Width: 70' - 0"
Depth: 44' - 0"
Foundation: Unfinished Basement

ORDER ONLINE @ EPLANS.COM

Stone, stucco and a combination of gables and arches create a stunning elevation on this elegant home. The two-story entry reveals French doors to the spider-beam library, an ideal room for business, study, or relaxation. The formal area to the right features an arched transom window in the living room and French doors from the dining room into the kitchen. Here, the family gourmet will revel in an expansive island with a triple cooktop, a snack bar, wrapping counters, and a built-in desk. The bayed breakfast area provides a pleasant eating space, and the nearby family room glows with the warmth of a fireplace. Upstairs, the sleeping zone includes three family bedrooms sharing two baths, plus an exquisite master suite with a bayed sitting area, a large walk-in closet, an oval whirlpool tub, His and Hers vanities, and a spacious shower with glass-block details.

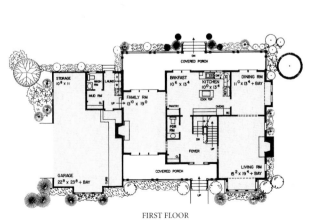

FIRST FLOOR

SECOND FLOOR

THIRD FLOOR

Named for the architect Henry Hobson Richardson, Richardson Romanesque homes are known for being ample in size and substantial in appearance. This three-story example is indicative of the style's best characteristics. Complementary arches on the outside lead to a wonderfully convenient floor plan. Formal and informal living areas occupy the first floor in a living room, a dining room, a family room, and a grand country kitchen. Upstairs are two family bedrooms and a lavish master suite with a sitting area. The third floor contains another bedroom and a private bath that could serve guests or live-ins quite well. Full-width verandas, front and back, provide indoor/outdoor living relationships and add just the right Victorian touch.

plan⊕ HPK2800195

First Floor: 1,405 sq. ft.
Second Floor: 1,430 sq. ft.
Third Floor: 624 sq. ft.
Total: 3,459 sq. ft.
Bedrooms: 4
Bathrooms: 3 ½
Width: 62' - 4"
Depth: 51' - 4"
Foundation: Unfinished Basement

ORDER ONLINE @ EPLANS.COM

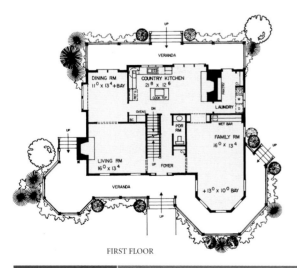

FIRST FLOOR

SECOND FLOOR

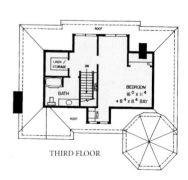

THIRD FLOOR

HELPFUL HINT! Garages and porches are never calculated in the total square footage of a home.

Another design that borrows from the forceful style of Henry Hobson Richardson, this home features a rounded turret top and rounded arches on the turret's windows. The interior allows plenty of room for busy lifestyles. Besides formal living and dining rooms and a casual family gathering room, there is a study with a corner fireplace that also serves as a media room. Three bedrooms are found on the second floor along with two full baths. The third floor contains another bedroom with a full bath and a small alcove. Wide verandas both front and rear, and a screened porch just off the family room allow good indoor/outdoor living relationships. Be sure to check-out the large hobby/laundry area connecting the house to the garage.

plan# HPK2800194

First Floor: 2,393 sq. ft.
Second Floor: 1,703 sq. ft.
Third Floor: 716 sq. ft.
Total: 4,812 sq. ft.
Bedrooms: 4
Bathrooms: 3½ + 3½
Width: 100' - 0"
Depth: 48' - 0"
Foundation: Unfinished Basement

ORDER ONLINE @ EPLANS.COM

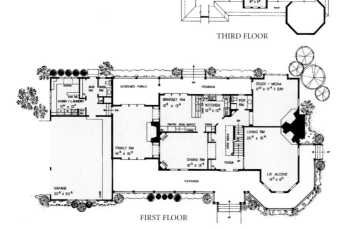

FIRST FLOOR

THIRD FLOOR

SECOND FLOOR

Reminiscent of the Gothic Victorian style of the mid-19th Century, this delightfully detailed three-story house presents a wraparound veranda for summertime relaxing. A grand reception hall welcomes visitors and displays an elegant staircase. The parlor and family room, each with a fireplace, provide excellent formal and informal living facilities. The well-planned kitchen is only a couple of steps from the dining and breakfast rooms. The family room and the breakfast room both provide access to the rear terrace. The second floor holds four bedrooms and two baths plus a sewing room or a study. The third floor houses an additional bedroom or a studio with a half-bath, as well as a playroom.

plan# HPK2800196

First Floor: 1,599 sq. ft.
Second Floor: 1,055 sq. ft.
Third Floor: 911 sq. ft.
Total: 3,565 sq. ft.
Bedrooms: 5
Bathrooms: 2½ + ½
Width: 88' - 0"
Depth: 42' - 0"
Foundation: Unfinished Basement

ORDER ONLINE @ EPLANS.COM

THIRD FLOOR

SECOND FLOOR

FIRST FLOOR

plan# HPK2800197

First Floor: 1,983 sq. ft.
Second Floor: 1,892 sq. ft.
Total: 3,875 sq. ft.
Bedrooms: 4
Bathrooms: 3½
Width: 72' - 8"
Depth: 49' - 8"
Foundation: Unfinished Basement

ORDER ONLINE @ EPLANS.COM

The striking Gothic exterior of this home conceals a floor plan designed for 20th-century livability. The large foyer features a dramatic curving staircase to the second floor. Formal living areas are located to the front of the plan; informal living areas are to the rear. The large formal dining room includes a delightful bay window. The formal living room is spacious and opens through a pleasingly detailed and columned archway to the cheerful music room. The rear, U-shaped kitchen features an island work surface and a walk-in pantry. The adjacent breakfast nook accesses the rear covered porch through sliding glass doors. Four bedrooms, three baths, and a huge library/playroom grace the upstairs. The master bedroom caters to the owners with individual sinks and walk-in closets, a separate vanity area, and a whirlpool tub.

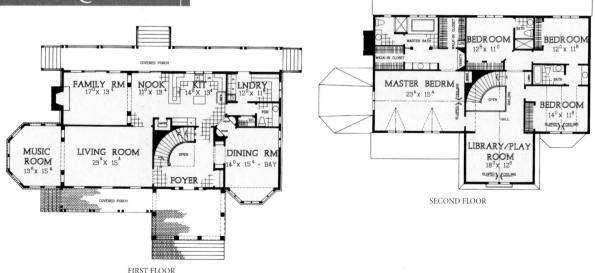

FIRST FLOOR

SECOND FLOOR

From lovely covered front porch to classic rear veranda, this three-story Folk Victorian offers the finest in modern floor plans. The formal living areas are set off by a family room which connects the main house to the service areas. The laundry has room for not only a washer and dryer but also a freezer and sewing area. The second floor holds three bedrooms and two full baths. A sitting area in the master suite separates it from family bedrooms. On the third floor is a guest bedroom with gracious bath and large walk-in closet, plus a large storage area.

plan# HPK2800198

First Floor: 1,531 sq. ft.
Second Floor: 1,307 sq. ft.
Third Floor: 664 sq. ft.
Total: 3,502 sq. ft.
Bedrooms: 4
Bathrooms: 3½
Width: 70' - 0"
Depth: 40' - 0"
Foundation: Unfinished Basement

ORDER ONLINE @ EPLANS.COM

THIRD FLOOR

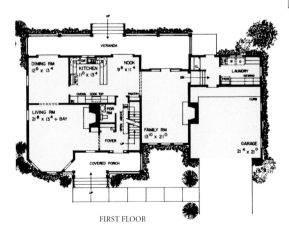

FIRST FLOOR

SECOND FLOOR

This charming Victorian home is reminiscent of a time when letter writing was an art and the scent of lavender hung lightly in the air. However, the floor plan moves quickly into the present with a contemporary flair. A veranda wraps around the living room, providing entrance from each side. The hub of the first floor is a kitchen that serves the dining room, the family room, and the living room with equal ease. Located on the second floor are two family bedrooms, a full bath, and an opulent master suite. Amenities in this suite include a fireplace, a bay-windowed sitting room, a pampering master bath, and a private sundeck. The third floor holds two bedrooms—one a possible study—and a full bath.

THIRD FLOOR

SECOND FLOOR

FIRST FLOOR

This home is perfect for a narrow in-fill lot in a neighborhood with an architectural history. A simple but charming Queen Anne Victorian, this enchanting three-story home includes a living room with a fireplace, a large family kitchen with a snack bar and a second fireplace, and a dining room with a nearby wet bar. The second floor holds two bedrooms, one a master suite with a grand bath. A tucked-away guest suite on the third floor has a private bath.

plan # HPK2800200

First Floor: 1,366 sq. ft.
Second Floor: 837 sq. ft.
Third Floor: 363 sq. ft.
Total: 2,566 sq. ft.
Bedrooms: 3
Bathrooms: 3½
Width: 47' - 4"
Depth: 65' - 10"
Foundation: Unfinished Basement

ORDER ONLINE @ EPLANS.COM

THIRD FLOOR

SECOND FLOOR

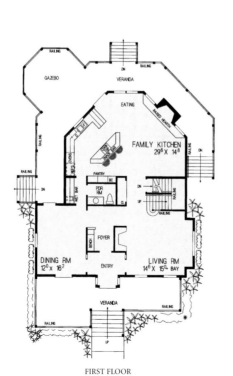

FIRST FLOOR

plan# HPK2800201

First Floor: 1,844 sq. ft.
Second Floor: 1,546 sq. ft.
Total: 3,390 sq. ft.
Bedrooms: 4
Bathrooms: 3
Width: 39' - 7"
Depth: 61' - 10"
Foundation: Slab

ORDER ONLINE @ EPLANS.COM

This outstanding home adds just the right measure of Victorian charm. Two porches and an upper terrace provide a variety of outside areas. The two-story cupola-style tower forms bay windows in the parlor near the formal dining room downstairs and in the sitting area in the master bedroom above. An open circular staircase, a fireplace in the family room, and a bay window in the breakfast room are some of the charming features in this classic Queen Anne design. Four bedrooms, three bathrooms, and a well-designed kitchen complete this delightful home.

SECOND FLOOR

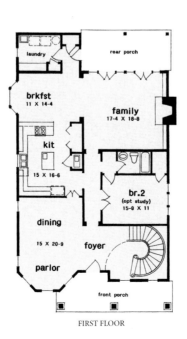

FIRST FLOOR

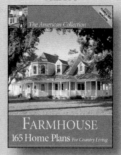

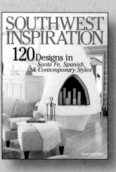

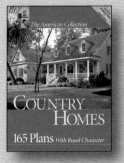
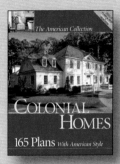

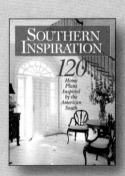

hanley▲wood
SELECTION, CONVENIENCE, SERVICE!

With more than 50 years of experience in the industry and millions of blueprints sold, Hanley Wood is a trusted source of high-quality, high-value pre-drawn home plans.

Using pre-drawn home plans is a **reliable, cost-effective way** to build your dream home, and our vast selection of plans is second-to-none. The nation's finest designers craft these plans that builders know they can trust. Meanwhile, our friendly, knowledgeable customer service representatives can help you every step of the way.

WHAT YOU'LL GET WITH YOUR ORDER

The contents of each designer's blueprint package is unique, but all contain detailed, high-quality working drawings. You can expect to find the following standard elements in most sets of plans:

I. FRONT PERSPECTIVE
This artist's sketch of the exterior of the house gives you an idea of how the house will look when built and landscaped.

2. FOUNDATION AND BASEMENT PLANS
This sheet shows the foundation layout including concrete walls, footings, pads, posts, beams, bearing walls, and foundation notes. If the home features a basement, the first-floor framing details may also be included on this plan. If your plan features slab construction rather than a basement, the plan shows footings and details for a

monolithic slab. This page, or another in the set, may include a sample plot plan for locating your house on a building site. Additional sheets focus on foundation cross-sections and other details.

3. DETAILED FLOOR PLANS
These plans show the layout of each floor of the house. Rooms and interior spaces are carefully dimensioned, doors and windows located, and keys are given for cross-section details provided elsewhere in the plans.

4. HOUSE AND DETAIL CROSS-SECTIONS
Large-scale views show sections or cutaways of the foundation, interior walls, exterior walls, floors, stairways, and roof details. Additional cross-sections may show important changes in floor, ceiling, or roof heights, or the relationship of one level to another. These sections show exactly how the various parts of the house fit together and are extremely valuable during construction. Additional sheets may include enlarged wall, floor, and roof construction details.

5. FLOOR STRUCTURAL SUPPORTS
The floor framing plans provide detail for these crucial elements of your home. Each includes floor joist, ceiling joist, spacing, direction, span, and specifications. Beam and window headers, along with necessary details for framing connections, stairways, or dormers are also included.

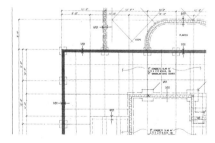

6. ELECTRICAL PLAN

The electrical plan offers suggested locations with notes for all lighting, outlets, switches, and circuits. A layout is provided for each level, as well as basements, garages, or other structures. This plan does not contain diagrams detailing how all wiring should be run, or how circuits should be engineered. These details should be designed by your electrician.

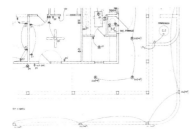

7. EXTERIOR ELEVATIONS

In addition to the front exterior, your blueprint set will include drawings of the rear and sides of your house as well. These drawings give notes on exterior materials and finishes. Particular attention is given to cornice detail, brick and stone accents, or other finish items that make your home unique.

ROOF FRAMING PLANS — PLEASE READ

Some plans contain roof framing plans; however because of the wide variation in local requirements, many plans do not. If you buy a plan without a roof framing plan, you will need an engineer familiar with local building codes to create a plan to build your roof. Even if your plan does contain a roof framing plan, we recommend that a local engineer review the plan to verify that it will meet local codes.

BEFORE YOU CALL

You are making a terrific decision to use a pre-drawn house plan—it is one you can make with confidence, knowing that your blueprints are crafted by national-award-winning certified residential designers and architects, and trusted by builders.

Once you've selected the plan you want—or even if you have questions along the way—our experienced customer service representatives are available 24 hours a day, seven days a week to help you navigate the home-building process. To help them provide you with even better service, please consider the following questions before you call:

■ Have you chosen or purchased your lot?
If so, please review the building setback requirements of your local building authority before you call. You don't need to have a lot before ordering plans, but if you own land already, please have the width and depth dimensions handy when you call.

■ Have you chosen a builder?
Involving your builder in the plan selection and evaluation process may be beneficial. Luckily, builders know they can have confidence with pre-drawn plans because they've been designed for livability, functionality, and typically are builder-proven at successful home sites across the country.

■ Do you need a construction loan?
Construction loans are unique because they involve determining the value of something that is not yet constructed. Several lenders offer convenient contstruction-to-permanent loans. It is important to choose a good lending partner—one who will help guide you through the application and appraisal process. Most will even help you evaluate your contractor to ensure reliability and credit worthiness. Our partnership with IndyMac Bank, a nationwide leader in construction loans, can help you save on your loan, if needed (see the next page for details).

■ How many sets of plans do you need?
Building a home can typically require a number of sets of blueprints—one for yourself, two or three for the builder and subcontractors, two for the local building department, and one or

more for your lender. For this reason, we offer 5- and 8-set plan packages, but your best value is the Reproducible Plan Package. Reproducible plans are accompanied by a license to make modifications and typically up to 12 duplicates of the plan so you have enough copies of the plan for everyone involved in the financing and construction of your home.

■ Do you want to make any changes to the plan?
We understand that it is difficult to find blueprints for a home that will meet all of your needs. That is why Hanley Wood is glad to offer plan Customization Services. We will work with you to design the modifications you'd like to see and to adjust your blueprint plans accordingly—anything from changing the foundation; adding square footage, redesigning baths, kitchens, or bedrooms; or most other modifications. This simple, cost-effective service saves you from hiring an outside architect to make alterations. Modifications may only be made to Reproducible Plan Packages that include the license to modify.

■ Do you have to make any changes to meet local building codes?
While all of our plans are drawn to meet national building codes at the time they were created, many areas required that plans be stamped by a local engineer to certify that they meet local building codes. Building codes are updated frequently and can vary by state, county, city, or municipality. Contact your local building inspection department, office of planning and zoning, or department of permits to determine how your local codes will affect your construction project. The best way to assure that you can make changes to your plan, if necessary, is to purchase a Reproducible Plan Package.

■ Has everyone—from family members to contractors—been involved in selecting the plan?
Building a new home is an exciting process, and using pre-drawn plans is a great way to realize your dreams. Make sure that everyone involved has had an opportunity to review the plan you've selected. While Hanley Wood is the only plans provider with an exchange policy, it's best to be sure all parties agree on your selection before you buy.

CALL TOLL-FREE 1-800-521-6797

Source Key
HPK28

CUSTOMIZE YOUR PLAN –
HANLEY WOOD CUSTOMIZATION SERVICES

Creating custom home plans has never been easier and more directly accessible. Using state-of-the-art technology and top-performing architectural expertise, Hanley Wood delivers on a long-standing customer commitment to provide world-class home-plans and customization services. Our valued customers—professional home builders and individual home owners—appreciate the convenience and accessibility of this interactive, consultative service.

With the Hanley Wood Customization Service you can:

■ Save valuable time by avoiding drawn-out and frequently repetitive face-to-face design meetings

■ Communicate design and home-plan changes faster and more efficiently
■ Speed-up project turn-around time
■ Build on a budget without sacrificing quality
■ Transform master home plans to suit your design needs and unique personal style

All of our design options and prices are impressively affordable. A detailed quote is available for a $50 consultation fee. Plan modification is an interactive service. Our skilled team of designers will guide you through the customization process from start to finish making recommendations, offering ideas, and determining the feasibility of your changes. This level of service is offered to ensure the final modified plan meets your expectations. If you use our service the $50 fee will be applied to the cost of the modifications.

You may purchase the customization consultation before or after purchasing a plan. In either case, it is necessary to purchase the Reproducible Plan Package and complete the accompanying license to modify the plan before we can begin customization.

Customization Consultation $50

TOOLS TO WORK WITH YOUR BUILDER

Two Reverse Options For Your Convenience – Mirror and Right-Reading Reverse (as available)

Mirror reverse plans simply flip the design 180 degrees—keep in mind, the text will also be flipped. For a minimal fee you can have one or all of your plans shipped mirror reverse, although we recommend having at least one regular set handy. Right-reading reverse plans show the design flipped 180 degrees but the text reads normally. When you choose this option, we ship each set of purchased blueprints in this format.

Mirror Reverse Fee (indicate the number of sets when ordering) $55
Right Reading Reverse Fee (all sets are reversed) $175

A Shopping List Exclusively for Your Home – Materials List

A customized Materials List helps you plan and estimate the cost of your new home, outlining the quantity, type, and size of materials needed to build your house (with the exception of mechanical system items). Included are framing lumber, windows and doors, kitchen and bath cabinetry, rough and finished hardware, and much more.

Materials List . . . .$85 each
Additional Materials Lists (at original time of purchase only)$20 each

Plan Your Home-Building Process – Specification Outline

Work with your builder on this step-by-step chronicle of 166 stages or items crucial to the building process. It provides a comprehensive review of the construction process and helps you choose materials.
Specification Outline . . . .$10 each

Get Accurate Cost Estimates for Your Home – Quote One® Cost Reports

The Summary Cost Report, the first element in the Quote One® package, breaks down the cost of your home into various categories based on building materials, labor, and installation, and includes three grades of construction: Budget, Standard, and Custom. Make even more informed decisions about your project with the second element of our package, the Material Cost Report. The material and installation cost is shown for each of more than 1,000 line items provided in the standard-grade Materials List, which is included with this tool. Additional space is included for estimates from contractors and subcontractors, such as for mechanical materials, which are not included in our packages.

Quote One® Summary Cost Report $35
Quote One® Detailed Material Cost Report $140*
***Detailed material cost report includes the Materials List**

Learn the Basics of Building – Electrical, Pluming, Mechanical, Construction Detail Sheets

If you want to know more about building techniques—and deal more confidently with your subcontractors—we offer four useful detail sheets. These sheets provide non-plan-specific general information, but are excellent tools that will add to your understanding of Plumbing Details, Electrical Details, Construction Details, and Mechanical Details.

Electrical Detail Sheet $14.95
Plumbing Detail Sheet $14.95
Mechanical Detail Sheet $14.95
Construction Detail Sheet $14.95
SUPER VALUE SETS:
Buy any 2: $26.95; Buy any 3: $34.95; Buy All 4: $39.95

Best Value

MAKE YOUR HOME TECH-READY – HOME AUTOMATION UPGRADE

Building a new home provides a unique opportunity to wire it with a plan for future needs. A Home Automation-Ready (HA-Ready) home contains the wiring substructure of tomorrow's connected home. It means that every room—from the front porch to the backyard, and from the attic to the basement—is wired for security, lighting, telecommunications, climate control, home computer networking, whole-house audio, home theater, shade control, video surveillance, entry access control, and yes, video gaming electronic solutions.

Along with the conveniences HA-Ready homes provide, they also have a higher resale value. The Consumer Electronics Association (CEA), in conjunction with the Custom Electronic Design and Installation Association (CEDIA), have developed a TechHome™ Rating system that quantifies the value of HA-Ready homes. The rating system is gaining widespread recognition in the real estate industry.

Developed by CEDIA-certified installers, our Home Automation Upgrade package includes everything you need to work with an installer during the construction of your home. It provides a short explanation of the various subsystems, a wiring floor plan for each level of your home, a detailed materials list with estimated costs, and a list of CEDIA-certified installers in your local area.
Home Automation Upgrade $250

GET YOUR HOME PLANS PAID FOR!

IndyMac Bank, in partnership with Hanley Wood, will reimburse you up to $1,000 toward the cost of your home plans simply by financing the construction of your new home with IndyMac Bank Home Construction Lending.

IndyMac's construction and permanent loan is a one-time close loan, meaning that one application—and one set of closing fees—provides all the financing you need.

Apply today at www.indymacbank.com, call toll free at 1-800-847-6138, or ask a Hanley Wood customer service representative for details.

DESIGN YOUR HOME – INTERIOR AND EXTERIOR FINISHING TOUCHES

Be Your Own Interior Designer! – Home Furniture Planner

Effectively plan the space in your home using our Hands-On Home Furniture Planner. It's fun and easy—no more moving heavy pieces of furniture to see how the room will go together. The kit includes reusable peel-and-stick furniture templates that fit on a 12"x18" laminated layout board—enough space to lay out every room in your house.
Home Furniture Planning Kit $15.95

Enjoy the Outdoors! – Deck Plans

Many of our homes have a corresponding deck plan, sold separately, which includes a Deck Plan Frontal Sheet, Deck Framing and Floor Plans, Deck Elevations, and a Deck Materials List. A Standard Deck Details Package, also available, provides all the how-to information necessary for building any deck. Get both the Deck Plan and the Standard Deck Details Package for one low price in our Complete Deck Building Package. See the price tier chart below and call for deck plan availability.
Deck Details (only) $14.95
Deck Building Package . . . . **Plan price + $14.95**

Create a Professionally Designed Landscape – Landscape Plans

Many of our homes have a front-yard Landscape Plan that is complementary in design to the house plan. These comprehensive Landscape Blueprint Packages include a Frontal Sheet, Plan View, Regionalized Plant & Materials List, a sheet on Planting and Maintaining Your Landscape, Zone Maps,  and a Plant Size and Description Guide. Each set of blueprints is a full 18" x 24" with clear, complete instructions in easy-to-read type. Our Landscape Plans are available with a Plant & Materials List adapted by horticultural experts to eight regions of the country. Please specify your region when ordering your plan—see region map below. Call for more information about landscape plan availability and applicable regions.

LANDSCAPE & DECK PRICE SCHEDULE

PRICE TIERS	1-SET STUDY PACKAGE	5-SET BUILDING PACKAGE	8-SET BUILDING PACKAGE	1-SET REPRODUCIBLE*
P1	$25	$55	$95	$145
P2	$45	$75	$115	$165
P3	$75	$105	$145	$195
P4	$105	$135	$175	$225
P5	$175	$205	$305	$405
P6	$215	$245	$345	$445

PRICES SUBJECT TO CHANGE   * REQUIRES A FAX NUMBER

TERMS & CONDITIONS

OUR 90-DAY EXCHANGE POLICY

Hanley Wood is committed to ensuring your satisfaction with your blueprint order, which is why we offer a 90-day exchange policy. With the exception of Reproducible Plan Package orders, we will exchange your entire first order for an equal or greater number of blueprints from our plan collection within 90 days of the original order. The entire content of your original order must be returned before an exchange will be processed. Please call our customer service department at 1-888-690-1116 for your return authorization number and shipping instructions. If the returned blueprints look used, redlined, or copied, we will not honor your exchange. Fees for exchanging your blueprints are as follows: 20% of the amount of the original order, plus the difference in cost if exchanging for a design in a higher price bracket or less the difference in cost if exchanging for a design in a lower price bracket. (Because they can be copied, Reproducible blueprints are not exchangeable or refundable.) Please call for current postage and handling prices. Shipping and handling charges are not refundable.

BUY WITH CONFIDENCE!

ARCHITECTURAL AND ENGINEERING SEALS

Some cities and states now require that a licensed architect or engineer review and "seal" a blueprint, or officially approve it, prior to construction. Prior to application for a building permit or the start of actual construction, we strongly advise that you consult your local building official who can tell you if such a review is required.

LOCAL BUILDING CODES AND ZONING REQUIREMENTS

Each plan was designed to meet or exceed the requirements of a nationally recognized model building code in effect at the time and place the plan was drawn. Typically plans designed after the year 2000 conform to the International Residential Building Code (IRC 2000 or 2003). The IRC is comprised of portions of the three major codes below. Plans drawn before 2000 conform to one of the three recognized building codes in effect at the time: Building Officials and Code Administrators (BOCA) International, Inc.;

the Southern Building Code Congress International, (SBCCI) Inc.; the International Conference of Building Officials (ICBO); or the Council of American Building Officials (CABO).

Because of the great differences in geography and climate throughout the United States and Canada, each state, county, and municipality has its own building codes, zone requirements, ordinances, and building regulations. Your plan may need to be modified to comply with local requirements. In addition, you may need to obtain permits or inspections from local governments before and in the course of construction. We authorize the use of the blueprints on the express condition that you consult a local licensed architect or engineer of your choice prior to beginning construction and strictly comply with all local building codes, zoning requirements, and other applicable laws, regulations, ordinances, and requirements. Notice: Plans for homes to be built in Nevada must be redrawn by a Nevada-registered professional. Consult your local building official for more information on this subject.

TERMS AND CONDITIONS

These designs are protected under the terms of United States Copyright Law and may not be copied or reproduced in any way, by

any means, unless you have purchased a Reproducible Plan Package and signed the accompanying license to modify and copy the plan, which clearly indicates your right to modify, copy, or reproduce. We authorize the use of your chosen design as an aid in the construction of ONE (1) single- or multifamily home only. You may not use this design to build a second dwelling or multiple dwellings without purchasing another blueprint or blueprints or paying additional design fees. Multi-use fees vary by designer—please call one of experienced sales representatives for a quote.

DISCLAIMER

The designers we work with have put substantial care and effort into the creation of their blueprints. However, because we cannot provide on-site consultation, supervision, and control over actual construction, and because of the great variance in local building requirements, building practices, and soil, seismic, weather, and other conditions, WE MAKE NO WARRANTY OF ANY KIND, EXPRESS OR IMPLIED, WITH RESPECT TO THE CONTENT OR USE OF THE BLUEPRINTS, INCLUDING BUT NOT LIMITED TO ANY WARRANTY OF MERCHANTABILITY OR OF FITNESS FOR A PARTICULAR PURPOSE. ITEMS, PRICES, TERMS, AND CONDITIONS ARE SUBJECT TO CHANGE WITHOUT NOTICE.

**CALL TOLL-FREE
1-800-521-6797
OR VISIT
EPLANS.COM**

IMPORTANT COPYRIGHT NOTICE

From the Council of Publishing Home Designers

Blueprints for residential construction (or working drawings, as they are often called in the industry) are copyrighted intellectual property, protected under the terms of the United States Copyright Law and, therefore, cannot be copied legally for use in building. The following are some guidelines to help you get what you need to build your home, without violating copyright law:

1. HOME PLANS ARE COPYRIGHTED

Just like books, movies, and songs, home plans receive protection under the federal copyright laws. The copyright laws prevent anyone, other than the copyright owner, from reproducing, modifying, or reusing the plans or design without permission of the copyright owner.

2. DO NOT COPY DESIGNS OR FLOOR PLANS FROM ANY PUBLICATION, ELECTRONIC MEDIA, OR EXISTING HOME

It is illegal to copy, change, or redraw home designs found in a plan book, CDROM or on the Internet. The right to modify plans is one of the exclusive rights of copyright. It is also illegal to copy or redraw a constructed home that is protected by copyright, even if you have never seen the plans for the home. If you find a plan or home that you like, you must purchase a set of plans from an authorized source. The plans may not be lent, given away, or sold by the purchaser.

3. DO NOT USE PLANS TO BUILD MORE THAN ONE HOUSE

The original purchaser of house plans is typically licensed to build a single home from the plans. Building more than one home from the plans without permission is an infringement of the home designer's copyright. The purchase of a multiple-set package of plans is for the construction of a single home only. The purchase of additional sets of plans does not grant the right to construct more than one home.

4. HOUSE PLANS IN THE FORM OF BLUEPRINTS OR BLACKLINES CANNOT BE COPIED OR REPRODUCED

Plans, blueprints, or blacklines, unless they are reproducibles, cannot be copied or reproduced without prior written consent of the copyright owner. Copy shops and blueprinters are prohibited from making copies of these plans without the copyright release letter you receive with reproducible plans.

5. HOUSE PLANS IN THE FORM OF BLUEPRINTS OR BLACKLINES CANNOT BE REDRAWN

Plans cannot be modified or redrawn without first obtaining the copyright owner's permission. With your purchase of plans, you are licensed to make non-structural changes by "red-lining" the purchased plans. If you need to make structural changes or need to redraw the plans for any reason, you must purchase a reproducible set of plans (see topic 6) which includes a license to modify the plans. Blueprints do not come with a license to make structural changes or to redraw the plans. You may not reuse or sell the modified design.

6. REPRODUCIBILE HOME PLANS

Reproducible plans (for example sepias, mylars, CAD files, electronic files, and vellums) come with a license to make modifications to the plans. Once modified, the plans can be taken to a local copy shop or blueprinter to make up to 10 or 12 copies of the plans to use in the construction of a single home. Only one home can be constructed from any single purchased set of reproducible plans either in original form or as modified. The license to modify and copy must be completed and returned before the plan will be shipped.

7. MODIFIED DESIGNS CANNOT BE REUSED

Even if you are licensed to make modifications to a copyrighted design, the modified design is not free from the original designer's copyright. The sale or reuse of the modified design is prohibited. Also, be aware that any modification to plans relieves the original designer from liability for design defects and voids all warranties expressed or implied.

8. WHO IS RESPONSIBLE FOR COPYRIGHT INFRINGEMENT?

Any party who participates in a copyright violation may be responsible including the purchaser, designers, architects, engineers, drafters, homeowners, builders, contractors, sub-contractors, copy shops, blueprinters, developers, and real estate agencies. It does not matter whether or not the individual knows that a violation is being committed. Ignorance of the law is not a valid defense.

9. PLEASE RESPECT HOME DESIGN COPYRIGHTS

In the event of any suspected violation of a copyright, or if there is any uncertainty about the plans purchased, the publisher, architect, designer, or the Council of Publishing Home Designers (www.cphd.org) should be contacted before proceeding. Awards are sometimes offered for information about home design copyright infringement.

10. PENALTIES FOR INFRINGEMENT

Penalties for violating a copyright may be severe. The responsible parties are required to pay actual damages caused by the infringement (which may be substantial), plus any profits made by the infringer commissions to include all profits from the sale of any home built from an infringing design. The copyright law also allows for the recovery of statutory damages, which may be as high as $150,000 for each infringement. Finally, the infringer may be required to pay legal fees which often exceed the damages.

BLUEPRINT PRICE SCHEDULE

PRICE TIERS	1-SET STUDY PACKAGE	5-SET BUILDING PACKAGE	8-SET BUILDING PACKAGE	1-SET REPRODUCIBLE*
A1	$465	$515	$570	$695
A2	$505	$560	$615	$755
A3	$570	$625	$685	$860
A4	$615	$680	$745	$925
C1	$660	$735	$800	$990
C2	$710	$785	$845	$1,055
C3	$775	$835	$900	$1,135
C4	$830	$905	$960	$1,215
L1	$920	$1,020	$1,105	$1,375
L2	$1,000	$1,095	$1,185	$1,500
L3	$1,105	$1,210	$1,310	$1,650
L4	$1,220	$1,335	$1,425	$1,830
SQ1				.40/SQ. FT.
SQ3				.55/SQ. FT.
SQ5				.80/SQ. FT.

PRICES SUBJECT TO CHANGE

* REQUIRES A FAX NUMBER

PLAN #	PRICE TIER	PAGE	MATERIALS LIST	QUOTE ONE®	DECK	DECK PRICE	LANDSCAPE	LANDSCAPE PRICE	REGIONS
HPK2800001	C2	6							
HPK2800002	A4	8							
HPK2800003	A3	12	Y						
HPK2800004	A3	13	Y						
HPK2800005	A3	14	Y						
HPK2800006	A3	15	Y						
HPK2800007	C1	16	Y						
HPK2800008	A3	17	Y						
HPK2800009	C1	18							
HPK2800010	C1	19							
HPK2800011	A4	20							
HPK2800012	A2	21							
HPK2800013	A3	22							
HPK2800014	A2	23							
HPK2800015	A2	24	Y						
HPK2800016	A3	24	Y						
HPK2800017	A4	25	Y						
HPK2800018	A4	26	Y						
HPK2800019	A4	27	Y						
HPK2800020	A3	28	Y						
HPK2800021	A3	29	Y						
HPK2800023	A2	30							
HPK2800022	A4	31	Y						
HPK2800024	C1	32	Y	Y	ODA011	D1	OLA093	P3	12345678
HPK2800025	A2	33							
HPK2800026	A4	34	Y	Y					
HPK2800028	A4	35	Y						
HPK2800029	A4	35	Y						
HPK2800030	A4	36	Y						
HPK2800031	A3	36	Y						
HPK2800032	A4	37	Y						
HPK2800033	A4	38	Y						
HPK2800034	A4	39	Y						
HPK2800027	A4	40	Y						
HPK2800035	A3	41	Y						
HPK2800036	A3	42	Y						

PLAN #	PRICE TIER	PAGE	MATERIALS LIST	QUOTE ONE®	DECK	DECK PRICE	LANDSCAPE	LANDSCAPE PRICE	REGIONS
HPK2800037	C1	44	Y						
HPK2800038	A4	45	Y						
HPK2800039	A4	46	Y						
HPK2800040	A4	47	Y						
HPK2800041	C1	48	Y	Y					
HPK2800042	C1	49	Y	Y					
HPK2800043	C1	50	Y	Y					
HPK2800044	A4	51	Y						
HPK2800045	A4	52	Y						
HPK2800047	SQ1	52	Y						
HPK2800046	SQ1	53	Y						
HPK2800048	A3	54							
HPK2800049	A4	55	Y						
HPK2800050	A4	56	Y						
HPK2800051	C1	57	Y				OLA001	P3	123568
HPK2800052	C2	58	Y						
HPK2800053	C4	58							
HPK2800054	A4	59	Y						
HPK2800055	A4	60	Y						
HPK2800056	C1	61	Y						
HPK2800057	C1	62	Y						
HPK2800058	C1	63	Y						
HPK2800059	C1	64	Y						
HPK2800060	C1	65	Y						
HPK2800061	SQ1	66	Y	Y			OLA010	P3	1234568
HPK2800062	A4	67	Y	Y			OLA024	P4	123568
HPK2800063	A4	68	Y		ODA011	D1	OLA025	P3	123568
HPK2800064	A4	69	Y						
HPK2800065	A4	69	Y						
HPK2800066	A4	70	Y						
HPK2800067	A4	71	Y						
HPK2800068	A4	72	Y						
HPK2800069	A4	73	Y						
HPK2800070	C3	74	Y						
HPK2800071	A4	75	Y						
HPK2800072	C1	76	Y						

PLAN #	PRICE TIER	PAGE	MATERIALS LIST	QUOTE ONE®	DECK	DECK PRICE	LANDSCAPE	LANDSCAPE PRICE	REGIONS
HPK2800073	A4	77	Y						
HPK2800074	C1	78	Y						
HPK2800075	A4	78	Y						
HPK2800076	SQ1	79	Y						
HPK2800077	A4	80							
HPK2800078	A4	80							
HPK2800079	A4	81							
HPK2800080	A4	82							
HPK2800081	A4	82							
HPK2800082	A4	83							
HPK2800083	C1	84							
HPK2800084	C1	84							
HPK2800085	C3	85							
HPK2800086	C2	86							
HPK2800087	C1	87							
HPK2800088	C1	87							
HPK2800089	C2	88	Y						
HPK2800090	C2	88							
HPK2800091	C2	89							
HPK2800092	C2	90							
HPK2800093	C2	91							
HPK2800095	A3	92							
HPK2800096	A4	93							
HPK2800097	C1	94							
HPK2800098	C1	95							
HPK2800094	A4	96							
HPK2800099	C1	98							
HPK2800100	C4	99							
HPK2800101	C1	100							
HPK2800102	C1	101							
HPK2800103	C1	102							
HPK2800104	C2	102							
HPK2800105	C1	103							
HPK2800106	C2	104							
HPK2800107	SQ1	105							
HPK2800108	C2	106				OLA004	P3	123568	
HPK2800109	SQ1	107	Y			OLA010	P3	1234568	
HPK2800110	C4	108							
HPK2800111	C1	109							
HPK2800112	C1	110							
HPK2800113	C3	111							
HPK2800114	C3	111	Y						
HPK2800115	C3	112	Y						
HPK2800116	C1	112							
HPK2800118	C3	113	Y						
HPK2800117	C3	114	Y						
HPK2800119	C1	114	Y						
HPK2800120	C1	115	Y						
HPK2800121	C1	116							
HPK2800122	C1	116							
HPK2800123	SQ1	117							
HPK2800124	C2	117							
HPK2800125	C3	118							
HPK2800126	C1	119							
HPK2800127	C1	120							
HPK2800128	C4	121							
HPK2800129	C4	121							
HPK2800130	C4	122							
HPK2800131	L2	123							
HPK2800132	C4	124							
HPK2800133	C4	124							
HPK2800134	L1	125							
HPK2800135	C2	126							
HPK2800136	C4	126	Y						
HPK2800137	C4	127							
HPK2800138	C2	128							
HPK2800139	C2	129							
HPK2800140	C1	129							
HPK2800141	C2	130							
HPK2800142	C2	130							
HPK2800143	C1	131							
HPK2800144	C4	132							
HPK2800145	C4	133							
HPK2800146	C3	133							
HPK2800147	C2	134	Y						
HPK2800148	C2	135	Y						
HPK2800149	C2	136	Y						
HPK2800150	C2	136	Y						
HPK2800151	C2	137	Y						
HPK2800152	C3	138	Y						
HPK2800153	C2	139	Y						
HPK2800154	C3	140							
HPK2800155	C3	140	Y						
HPK2800156	C3	141							
HPK2800157	C3	142							
HPK2800158	C4	143							
HPK2800159	C4	143							
HPK2800160	C3	144							
HPK2800161	C4	145							
HPK2800162	C3	146							
HPK2800163	C3	146	Y						
HPK2800164	C3	147	Y						
HPK2800165	C4	148	Y						
HPK2800166	C3	149							
HPK2800167	C4	150							
HPK2800168	C4	150							
HPK2800169	C4	151							
HPK2800170	C4	151							
HPK2800171	C3	152							
HPK2800172	C4	153	Y						
HPK2800173	C3	154							
HPK2800174	C3	154							
HPK2800175	L1	155							
HPK2800176	C4	156							
HPK2800177	C3	157							
HPK2800178	C1	158	Y						
HPK2800179	C1	159	Y						
HPK2800180	C1	160	Y						
HPK2800181	C1	161	Y						
HPK2800182	SQ1	162	Y						
HPK2800183	SQ1	163	Y						
HPK2800184	C1	164	Y						
HPK2800185	C1	165	Y						
HPK2800186	C1	166	Y						
HPK2800187	C2	167							
HPK2800188	L3	168	Y	Y			OLA008	P4	1234568
HPK2800189	C4	169	Y	Y	ODA012	D2	OLA024	P4	123568
HPK2800190	SQ1	170	Y		ODA011	D1	OLA024	P4	123568
HPK2800191	SQ1	171	Y	Y	ODA012	D2	OLA024	P4	123568
HPK2800192	L1	172	Y	Y	ODA012	D2	OLA017	P3	123568
HPK2800193	C4	173			ODA012	D2	OLA008	P4	1234568
HPK2800195	SQ1	174	Y	Y	ODA011	D1	OLA024	P4	123568
HPK2800194	C4	175	Y		ODA011	D1	OLA025	P3	123568
HPK2800196	C3	176	Y				OLA025	P3	123568
HPK2800197	L1	177	Y	Y	ODA011	D1	OLA024	P4	123568
HPK2800198	L1	178	Y	Y	ODA012	D2	OLA008	P4	123568
HPK2800199	C3	179	Y	Y			OLA024	P4	1234568
HPK2800200	SQ1	180	Y	Y	ODA011	D1	OLA003	P3	123568
HPK2800201	C3	181